SHASTA AND

Simon and Schuster / *New York*

ROBERT L. BEHME

ROGUE *A Coyote Story*

COPYRIGHT © 1974 BY ROBERT L. BEHME
ALL RIGHTS RESERVED
INCLUDING THE RIGHT OF REPRODUCTION
IN WHOLE OR IN PART IN ANY FORM
PUBLISHED BY SIMON AND SCHUSTER
ROCKEFELLER CENTER, 630 FIFTH AVENUE
NEW YORK, NEW YORK 10020

DESIGNED BY IRVING PERKINS
MANUFACTURED IN THE UNITED STATES OF AMERICA
PRINTED BY THE MURRAY PRINTING COMPANY, FORGE VILLAGE, MASS.
BOUND BY THE BOOK PRESS, BRATTLEBORO, VT.

1   2   3   4   5   6   7   8   9   10

LIBRARY OF CONGRESS CATALOGING IN PUBLICATION DATA

Behme, Robert Lee.
   Shasta and Rogue.
   1. Coyotes—Legends and stories.   I. Title.
   QL795.C6B37   818'.5'407   74-9673
          ISBN 0-671-21844-1

For Peggy

Shasta (LEFT) *and Rogue* (RIGHT) *the first day in our house. At the age of two and one-half weeks, their eyes were barely open, and vision was limited to a couple of feet.*

Chapter One

Heavy clouds scudded ominously across the sky as I eased the car down the steep, winding road. A fine snow fell lightly against the windshield and stuck white to the firs and pines that lined the road. Peggy turned beside me to inspect the contents of a cardboard box in the rear.

"They're cold," she said anxiously, and in the mirror I could see her holding two small, woolly animals. Their narrow muzzles poked at the air like thin, nervous fingers, and their fur, dark on the back and lighter on the tail, ended abruptly on the stomach. Their bellies were pink, hairless circles. I parked off the highway and held one animal awkwardly as Peggy wrapped the other in a towel. Our affair with coyotes had begun.

We live in northern California with our younger son, Erik. An older son, Malcolm, is in college near San Francisco. At the time the coyotes joined us, we were sharing our house with two more conventional pets—Elizabeth, an aging English bulldog who snuffles and snorts even as she sleeps, and Russell, a tiger cat.

Our home is in that part of the state called the Mother Lode, the historic gold country of the Forty-niners. Since 1850, men have scrambled across its face in search of ore, but our part is not like the richer areas farther south where big mines and big money have been discovered. Here there were many losers, and winning was simply a day-by-day struggle for survival. You can tell that from the things which remain.

The creek that flows past our patio was rerouted a hundred and twenty years ago so that men could take ore from its bed. No one became rich, there is no more gold and all that remains of the change is a moss-covered rock wall. A century-old mine lies deserted in our backyard. As the men who dug it worked deeper they struck an underground stream and were flooded out before they came close to ore. We have it enclosed to keep children away.

Twelve miles from our home is a canyon in which the world's largest gold nugget was discovered. It was a fifty-pound boulder. The find was such an event that every year the people in our community celebrate "Golden Nugget Day" with a parade, costumes and a donkey race. It makes no difference that the nugget and the men who unearthed it are forgotten. Yet if this is not a rich area, the men who came for gold tried just as hard as they did in the south, and something of their sweat and hope remains. You can feel it.

Our home is surrounded by a thick, silent forest of pine and fir dotted with clusters of maple, and there are stands of alder where there is water. It is second-growth timber, but the trees are tall and the land is much as it might have been in those earlier days. The forest gives us a measure of privacy, and its coolness is home for a variety of animals. I am a department editor for *Field & Stream* magazine, and animals have played an important part in my life. I have fed skunks and raccoons on our porch, and it was a squirrel that started me thinking about coyotes.

I found a half-dead baby squirrel in our drive. It was newly born and its eyes were not open. Neither the nest nor the mother was to be found, and I made a home of towels in an unused birdcage. I set my alarm clock for two and six each morning and fed the animal heated milk, and it grew. Three months later I released it in the brush beside our house, and the squirrel scampered off without a backward glance. The experience stimulated a desire for a similar relationship with a larger animal, and of all of the possibilities in California, coyotes interested me most. Peggy and Erik seemed to feel the same way.

A number of species of wolves originally inhabited the continent, but as settlers moved west to clear and farm the land their habitat shrank, their numbers diminished and most are now endangered. But one species, known to most of the people who have lived on this continent, has been cunning enough to survive and even prosper. The Aztecs respected him and called him *coytl*. Lewis and Clark, the first white Americans to see him, called him "burrowing dog," and early settlers called him "prairie dog." Biologists use the name *Canis latrans*, which means barking dog. He is all of this—our smallest native wolf, the one animal I wanted to know as I had known that squirrel.

It would be difficult. Wild animals are not easy to gentle. They have little reason to trust humans, and if trust comes, it develops slowly. But I hoped that Peggy, Erik and I could break through that fear if we found one young enough. If we could become substitute parents, my plan might work.

It was a matter of timing. Pups are whelped in late March and early April in the plateaus of the Sierra Nevada, and I called John Regitano in March. As manager of a regional business-promotional organization, the Shasta-Cascade Wonderland Association, John knew resort owners, guides, game managers and U.S. Forest Rangers. I had worked with him on magazine articles and knew that if anyone could locate a stray coyote pup, John would be the most likely.

A week later he called. John had discovered a young man named Fran Gordon. Gordon in turn had found a coyote den in a rocky outcropping. His presence had frightened the mother, and she would not return. The pups were alone, and Gordon had taken them to his house. He told John we could have as many as we wanted.

The Gordon home was just one hundred miles north of ours, and Peggy and I arrived at the white clapboard house at noon the next day. There was fresh snow on the ground, and heavy gray clouds in the north were threatening more. Fran and his parents met us at the door, and beyond them I saw four tiny pups tucked in a box beside a blazing oil heater. They were helpless and frightened, and after much indecision I chose two—a fluffy female because she seemed to boss the litter and a larger, handsome male because he hovered alone and lost in one corner. I weakened at the sight and could not have left the house without him. The Gordons agreed to care for the remaining animals.

It was snowing as we left the house, and somehow in the silence that comes with snow and the gray skies I suddenly felt that it would be impossible to raise two small wild animals. Neither Peggy nor I knew anything about coyote pups and it would be a difficult task just to keep them alive.

When I stopped at a service station for gas, the attendant saw them in the box. "Grown coyotes eat carrion, and all that rotten meat poisons the mother's milk," he said. He predicted the pups were badly diseased and would infect our pets when they met.

We had expected to hear trapper's tales and half-truths, but the fact that they were beginning so soon shocked me. The feeling of foreboding grew, and my uneasiness was not reduced when a veterinarian who examined the pups on our way home found them healthy and still gave us a warning. All wolves have a "wild streak" we could never control, he said. "You'll have to handle them 'hard' to even get them to mind," he added, "and after a year they'll go wild. Then you must get rid of them."

Almost everyone who saw the pups had some coyote story and some warning. When we arrived home, a friend called to insist that I kill the pups while there was still time. "I knew a family who raised one with a small child," he said gloomily. "One day the kid cut a finger and the animal smelled blood. It went mad. Nearly killed the child before the parents could separate them."

Even though it was impossible to believe the tales, I felt uneasy and uncertain. Coyotes are what they eat, but to the extent of becoming diseased? Stupid! The wild streak? An old wives' tale. Going mad over blood? The same. The problem was that there was a thread of plausibility in each story, the people believed them and I had no ready replies.

My uncertainty frightened Peggy, and she looked at the pups with a mixture of sadness and regret, as if she were afraid of what lay in store for them. We were not the first to raise wolves, but most people who had raised them had either chosen larger species or left no record. We had read the few books we could find and there were no helpful hints, no how-to-do-it information. We were on our own, and only my instincts told me that love for these small, frightened animals would carry us toward our goal. Instead of worrying about matters I could neither prove nor control, I worried about a confrontation between the pups and Elizabeth and Russell. Would our pets consider the coyotes as friends or intruders? I felt Russell would be the more difficult, since his predator instincts were active on birds, mice and ground squirrels. The pups were small and defenseless and he could easily kill them.

I put the coyotes in a tall cardboard box. Erik hovered over them with excitement, and our pets came quickly. Elizabeth took one half-

Erik painting the first box we provided for the coyotes. The box was tall so that they could not leap out.

interested sniff, snorted and walked to another corner, where she dozed contentedly. But Russell strode arrogantly forward, his tail flashing from side to side. He caught their scent several feet from the box and paused questioningly. His black nose tested the air, and he inched himself cautiously toward the box as if there were something dangerous inside. He put his feet on the side and pulled himself upright to peer over the top. I hovered close above him, anticipating trouble. One of the pups stirred, and Russell jerked away as if he had been bitten. He circled the box nervously from a safe distance, and I carried him back to see why he was acting strangely. As soon as I released him, he bolted away.

The coyotes were one third his size and quite defenseless, and I couldn't decide why he had run. Then I noticed a strange, musky odor from their box, a scent I had not been aware of before. I wondered if that could be the explanation. I had heard about such things, and I told Peggy, "If there is such a thing as a 'wild smell,' it might be this. It could explain Russell's panic." I am not certain I believed the theory then, or that I believe it completely now, but it could be one reason the pups were safe. In any event, the cat never bothered them.

We had planned for a single coyote, a male, and Erik had named him Rogue even before we had gone to the Gordons' to claim him. Since I had returned with two, we needed a name for the female, and after working through a long list of possibilities we discussed the best of them over dinner and settled for the name of the country in which our coyotes had been born. Erik lettered their names on the box—HOME OF MISSY SHASTA AND THE HON. ROGUE—and that seemed to make it official.

As I helped clear the table, it was time for their first feeding. I knew some wild babies would not drink bottled milk until it had the taste and consistency of their mother's milk, and that was often difficult to duplicate. When I had first fed the squirrel he had refused cow's milk, condensed milk and various combinations until a veterinarian told me to add a dash of Karo.

Peggy and I sat on the couch with towels tied around our necks and bottles of plain warmed milk in our hands. I held Rogue. His jaws were tightly closed and I could not force the nipple through his lips. I pushed, poked and shoved, but he refused to drink. Then a small bubble of milk dropped from the nipple, ran along his lips and settled in one corner of his mouth, and a second later a small, pink tongue followed it. He tasted the fluid, then began feeding, sucking at the bottle in quick, deep gulps. I had trouble with the angle of the bottle—one moment Rogue got nothing and the next he had too much—and by the time the bottle was half empty I was squeezing the sides to force milk through the nipple. Something was wrong; milk was running down Rogue's tiny black muzzle, and he was coughing and kicking. Beside me, Shasta was feeding calmly from Peggy's expert hand.

I wiped Rogue's face, and when they were both through feeding we let them explore the room. The two pups moved from the shelter of our feet cautiously, first side by side, then in different directions. Although their eyes were open, a film reduced their vision to a few inches. They bumped into chairs and rocked from side to side on shaky legs. Soon they were tired, and we picked them up. They fell asleep on our laps.

The first signs of diarrhea appeared the next morning, and when the condition grew worse we took them to our veterinarian, Dr. Henry Evers. He told us the condition was common to orphans. "It's caused by a change in the character of the milk and can be serious. It weakens the animals," he said. He gave us several medicines: a small pink pill to cure the diarrhea, a liquid vitamin and cod-liver oil as supplemental nourishment and a large capsule of white powder to replace lost intestinal bacteria.

"If the capsule is too large," Evers said, "just pour the powder on their tongues."

The procedure seemed unnecessarily difficult, but when Shasta took her medicine without complaint I relaxed. Rogue devoured his tablet, the vitamin and the cod-liver oil, and Peggy held him for the final stage, the white powder. I opened his mouth, and he clamped it against my finger. His jaws were rimmed with small, razor-sharp teeth, and I yelled with pain. The capsule spun across the floor, leaving a zigzag line of white. Shasta sniffed it without interest. I opened a second capsule, parted Rogue's jaws with greater respect and dashed the powder inside as rapidly as possible. Rogue closed his tiny jaws with a snap that sounded more like that of a crocodile than that of a baby pup, and Peggy lowered him to the floor. He looked up angrily at me and regurgitated at my feet as if that were his final answer.

Somehow we survived the daily medications, and by the end of the

Rough-and-tumble games taught them the practical tactics of fighting they'd later need in the wild.

week the pups were healthy and active. They would play for hours, tumbling across the floor like wrestlers. Shasta was always the aggressor and seemed to play the harder, squealing, tumbling and pushing until she had Rogue pinned down.

When I first heard him cry, I raced toward the pups certain Shasta had injured her brother. I expected to find him bitten, beaten and bloody, but when I saw them Shasta was standing over the upturned Rogue, feet apart in triumph, and Rogue was howling at the indignity.

The cardboard box was still their home. Neither animal could see above the rim, and Rogue, who was the larger, could barely touch the top with his outstretched paws. It was protection, and they felt secure.

Erik playing with the coyotes. As pups, they loved to climb over him.

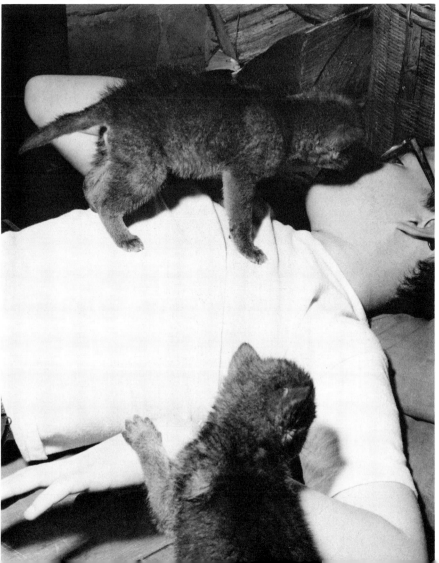

When the room was empty they played in the box, thumping and rolling against the sides, but when someone entered they became silent. I watched them for several hours and suddenly realized that this was instinctive. On the rocky ledge that had been their home, any noise would have given away the location of the den. They were quiet so that predators could not find them.

One morning I heard them playing and crept into the room. They heard my lightest footstep and stopped immediately. I could see them from across the room, although they could not see me. They were huddled at one end of the box, ears erect, heads moving from side to side like radar, trying to pinpoint the intrusion. When I came closer, they saw me and threw themselves against the box in a delighted welcome.

They were growing rapidly, with fat bodies and stiltlike legs that were completely out of proportion. The only part of their bodies resembling coyotes was their ears, and these were stiff, furry flags far larger than the scale of their heads. Their eyes were clearer, and they walked with a steadier step. They were awake longer and spent much of their time tearing apart their box. It was time to wean them.

I began with a shallow bowl of milk, but the liquid was difficult for them to handle. They could not lap, and we had to teach them. Peggy thickened the milk with baby cereal and lured Rogue with her finger dipped into the mixture. When he was eagerly licking her finger, she lowered it into the bowl, and he began eating. Shasta lowered her head and plopped her muzzle into the porridge. She struggled wildly to regain her footing, swinging her body unsteadily from side to side, finally lifting herself above the dish. Her muzzle was white with food, and she snorted, blowing milk and cereal in all directions.

The scene was repeated each time they ate, but we persisted. Every feeding began with cereal and milk and finished on our laps with bottles. Rogue was weaned on the third day, and on the fourth Shasta joined her brother.

"Now my kitchen can stay clean," Peggy said happily, but at the next meal Rogue pinned his dish with one paw set deep in the milk, and when he finished we could trace his route. A series of single white prints led from the dish like a dotted line.

The pups were becoming bolder, and it was inspiring to see the

A friend, Danny Larsen, feeding Shasta shortly after weaning.

Rogue inspects a book on the floor.

small, still defenseless animals strike into what was for them the unknown. They seemed to have the confidence to do anything and were eager to find new adventures. The living room was no longer the limit of their world. Each time we let them free they found something new, and we had to close doors to keep track of them. One day Shasta discovered the washing machine, and before we knew what she had in mind, she disappeared into it. I could hear her probing deeper and deeper into the motor compartment which backed against the wall.

"Stop worrying," Peggy said, "She'll find her way out." I was doubtful and hovered beside the machine like the parent of a lost child, and Rogue stood beside me, whining nervously. His call was answered by a single, lonely howl deep inside the machine. I was afraid to move

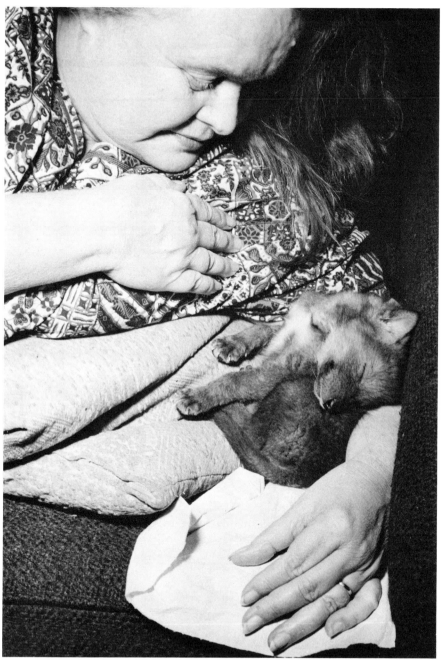

Shasta fell asleep in the arms of a visitor, Mrs. Arnoldine Small.

the heavy washer for fear the slightest movement would crush Shasta, yet I was equally certain she was too young to figure her way out.

After a long, uneasy silence I heard a thumping and bumping, and the noise wound around the case like someone tapping in the dark to find the way out of a tunnel. Suddenly the noise stopped and Shasta tumbled into the hall, covered with oil, grease and dust. Rogue fell on her with happiness, and Peggy cleaned her fur. I stuffed magazines around the washer to prevent a repetition of the event, and we put them in their box. The first three weeks had been busy ones.

Chapter Two

FEW OF OUR ACQUAINTANCES cared about coyotes. Most considered them varmints, animals to be slaughtered and exterminated, and friends who knew we had Shasta and Rogue thought we were crazy.

Perhaps coyotes have never been popular in America. A handful of men study them, most often to more effectively kill them; few raise them, and fewer write about them. We could find only three books in our public library. *The Clever Coyote*, by government biologists Stanley Young and Hartley Jackson, gave some insight into wild coyotes, but was essentially a primer for trappers—hardly our field. *The World of the Coyote*, by Joe Van Wormer, painted a broad picture of the way wild coyotes live and survive. The third, *The Voice of the Coyote*, was the most appealing. Written by J. Frank Dobie, famous for Western history, it was part fact, part fiction; entertaining, nostalgic and amusing and told of Dobie's love for the animals. Although the book offered no hints, nothing to help us raise our pups, it was reassuring to know that at least one writer shared our affection and concern. We were beginning to wonder if anyone did.

Shasta and Rogue were healthy, inquisitive and active, and while we could control them as well as we might have controlled domestic pups of a similar age, their abilities were different. Talents seemed to mushroom instinctively, full-blown and ready for use. It was as if they increased in size and skill before our eyes, and if we had doubts about our ability to raise them our uncertainty was more than balanced by the fascination that came from watching them develop. There was much that we did not understand.

One day Rogue discovered a plastic lid in the kitchen waste basket. He pulled it free before Peggy knew what was happening, dragged it to the center of the room and leaped on it. Rearing on his hindquarters like a stallion, he landed with his front legs stiff and straight, a motion he had never made before. He did it several times, and I could hear the sharp *whack, whack, whack* of his paws against the tile. I had seen photographs of full-grown coyotes catching field mice in an identical way and realized Rogue was learning a talent he must master to survive. The curious point: the technique was coming to him developed, recognizable and ready to use.

Later Shasta was poking at a cushion on our couch and suddenly began digging furiously, another action we had never seen before. She pushed a rubber ball into a space between two cushions, looked sideways to be certain Rogue was not watching and pushed folds of loose fabric over her cache with her nose as if the cloth were dirt. I could almost believe she was compelled by an outside force, and when she discovered what she could do she repeated her action several times to perfect the technique. Between distractions and other activities, she buried and retrieved the ball ten times that day.

At the age of one month the animals began to greet us occasionally with wagging tails held low, their mouths pulled into a shallow smile which exposed their small, sharp teeth. In the beginning I did not understand the gesture and could not tell whether they were being friendly or angry, challenging or playful. Later, I learned it was a natural action, one animal behaviorists call a "submissive grin." It was one way coyotes approach a leader and was, I supposed, flattering. At least it meant we were friends.

One Sunday, Erik growled. He hoped the sound would stimulate Rogue to play. The coyote sat on his haunches, cocked his head to one side and squinted. He was silent for several seconds, then opened his mouth and howled, and even though his voice was high-pitched and uncertain, the sound was authentically coyote. The two kept at the game for several minutes and Erik tired first. For some reason, Shasta would

Shasta would hide valuable items in odd corners of our house, such as this one, retrieving them later.

have no part of it. She circled nervously and kept her distance.

On one hand, the coyotes were maturing faster than their few weeks of life might indicate, but on the other, when faced with strange objects or new routines they were still small, frightened puppies demanding our security and reassurance. They were too young to care for themselves, and this was at the root of one of our most serious conflicts: travel.

I was working on a book about bonsai, miniature Japanese trees grown in pots. In the process of illustrating it, I drove throughout the West to photograph particularly good specimens. I worked alone most of the time, because it was difficult to bring Peggy and Erik, but I was

We took the pups to snow about a mile from our home. It was their first experience with it, and at first they were very cautious.

generally lonely, and when the coyotes were four weeks old I had an appointment in Sacramento, the state capital. I decided to take my family. We would dine at a restaurant, see a motion picture and stay the night at a motel—and in a moment of madness, I decided we could do all these things if we brought the pups. I could smuggle them into our motel room. The deception seemed harmless, since they spent much of their time in a box and I was certain they would be sufficiently awed by strange surroundings to be still and silent. The idea seemed practical, and I would have bet money on its success.

When I signed the register, I discovered that the only available room was above the office. Its location made me uneasy, and I should have reconsidered, but we were late for dinner and I did not want to search for

Peggy brings them back to the car. We wanted the coyotes to become accustomed to traveling at an early age. The results were not always successful.

another room. I took the room key and returned to the car. Erik was delighted at the prospect of an adventure.

I carried the coyote box under one arm, the pups rattling inside, and added a camera case beneath the other to buttress the illusion that I carried only harmless equipment. I passed the office without notice, went upstairs and put the pups in our bathroom; then we unpacked and dressed for dinner. They were a picture of peacefulness, curled calmly in one corner of their box, and were nearly asleep when I shut the bathroom door. I began to believe everything would be all right.

When we returned, much later, the pups met us at the entry, leaping eagerly in welcome. Beyond, I could see the open bathroom door and evidence of a delightful evening: cardboard torn from their box had been mixed with shredded newspaper and drinking water, and the sodden mess had been scattered around the room. The effect was one of total destruction—a tornado, a hurricane or an explosion. Erik scooped the coyotes into his arms and sat on the bed laughing hysterically as Peggy and I picked up the pieces.

Peggy asked, "What is our next step?"

"Put them in the bathroom again and make sure the door is closed and locked," I said grimly.

We readied ourselves for bed as the pups scampered freely around us; then I herded them into the bathroom, shut the door and made certain it was closed. There was no protest. The coyotes seemed calm, quiet and secure, almost as if they had worn themselves out with the earlier games. I turned off the light and relaxed in bed. We had been lucky: apparently the motel manager had not heard them. I was drifting to sleep when the scratching began. It grew louder, insistent and unmistakable, and when they began whining Erik burst into laughter.

"It's not funny," I fumed. "Do you want to spend the rest of the night in a car loaded with coyotes?"

Erik could not control himself, and when one of the pups cried—a loud, heartbreaking yip—Erik's laughter erupted, and Peggy giggled. "They'll soon tire of that," she said.

She was right. The whining stopped as suddenly as it had begun, replaced now by the click of claws across linoleum. There were sounds like a typewriter, and I stiffened. The coyotes were playing. There was no way the manager could miss such obviously audible noises directly above his head.

Then Rogue screamed, as if badly injured, and I raced to the bathroom, flung open the door and stepped inside the darkened room. My feet sank into a mixture of water, urine and wet paper as Shasta and Rogue sloshed joyously around me. Peggy switched on the light, and the front of my pajamas showed the distinct, clear pattern of paw prints.

We cleaned the room a second time, put the pups in their box, closed the door and turned off the light. The scratching, whining and running resumed. There was nothing more to do. I could not put them in the car; if I did, there would be little of it left by morning. And I could not open the bathroom door; if I did, there would be no sleep for us. I could only leave them as they were and wait tensely for daylight or the manager, whichever came first.

An hour after sunrise I awoke groggily. There were no sounds. All was quiet in the bedroom. I couldn't remember when they had stopped, but I shook Peggy gently and we began to dress as silently as possible. The coyotes heard us and in seconds were at the door scratching for attention. We let them out and again faced a bathroom that resembled a war zone. Pieces of cardboard and puddles of water pockmarked the floor like bomb craters. We finished dressing and cleaned the bathroom a third time as Erik kept the pups occupied.

After loading luggage and cameras in the car, I came back for the coyotes. The sides of their box were substantially shorter than they had been when we arrived, having been torn, trimmed, nibbled and manicured during the night. Shasta and Rogue could poke their heads above the top as often as they wished. They were inquisitive, and it would be hard to hide them on the trek to the car. Against protests, I spread my coat over them, stuffing flashbulb cartons around the edges for authenticity. I lifted the box like an armload of wood and started down the steps.

The motel manager was standing in the parking lot near our car, and for one moment, when he looked up, I thought he was waiting for me. I finally decided he was simply out for sun—but when Rogue poked his head from beneath the coat and peered anxiously down the stairs, I sucked in my breath and felt an empty, hollow response inside. I stuffed

*When Erik caught this good-sized trout from the stream near our home,
Rogue came immediately to inspect it.*

him hastily under cover and wondered how I could fake my way across the parking lot. As if on cue, two automobiles crashed at the intersection and an argument erupted between the drivers. The motel manager ambled toward the action, and I raced to my car, the box bouncing wildly from one arm to the other. I reached the door, opened it and flung the box onto the seat just as Shasta toppled from one side. I slammed the door and leaned against the trunk for one moment to thank God for success.

A week later, travel was again a problem. I had to make photographs in San Francisco, and Peggy wanted to do some shopping. I was in favor of another family outing, but insisted the coyotes be boarded at a veterinarian's. They would be well cared for and, I reasoned, the vet could guarantee that there would be no repeat of what I now remembered painfully as "the motel incident."

Again, my plan failed. We worried about the coyotes. We knew that without us a kennel could be a frightening place for small wild animals, and the problem was that no one quite knew how they would react. In the end we returned early, and as we waited for them at the kennel office I only hoped our fears were groundless. The attendant returned with a cardboard box held stiffly from his body as if it held something dangerously contaminated.

He said, "I kept them separated—on the quiet side, you could say— because I knew they were wild, but I don't think they appreciated it." We could hear the "quiet side"—a back room filled with yapping, howling dogs.

He put the box on the counter and backed away. A small hole had been cut in one side, and through it I could see Shasta and Rogue huddled nervously in the farthest corner. Their eyes were wide with fear, their hair was matted and they were shaking, and when Peggy approached they bared their teeth, hissing angrily like cats. We were shocked. Had they forgotten us?

I called their names. For one moment neither animal responded. Then Shasta blinked and leaped forward, and Rogue was close behind. Then they were on the counter, wiggling happily and licking our hands and arms, and we held them close before I put them into the car. On the drive home, Shasta leaped from the back seat to Peggy's arms in an endless circle, and Rogue ran between our seats. Suddenly he began to howl with delight, and Shasta joined in. It was the first time we had heard her howl, and her voice was an octave above Rogue's. The din was overwhelming.

"All right, all right," I shouted. "We'll never leave you alone again."

They had outgrown their box and a temporary pen on the porch and were too adventurous to run free. The only solution was an enclosed run, and I built one at the rear of our property. They came into the house for meals and play and soon established a trail from the back door through the hall to the kitchen, where they were fed. They were aware of everything en route and as long as all objects were in place came to their meals calmly. But when something was missing or replaced they noticed the change immediately and circled nervously, sometimes for an hour or more.

One evening I cooked steak and left the barbecue to cool on the deck behind the dining room. After dinner we let the coyotes into the house. They raced down the hall and pulled to an unexpected halt in the living room. Rogue looked apprehensively at the ceiling, out the door and back to the ceiling as if he expected danger to strike from the rafters, and Shasta paced anxiously. Neither animal would touch the food which stood in two pans near the glass door to the deck.

Erik suggested that the barbecue might be the problem. It had never before been on the porch, and I went outside to move it. There seemed no other reasonable explanation. I lifted the mushroomlike cooker, and two of its metal legs clattered to the deck. As I tried to balance the unit on one leg while I retrieved the others, it hung momentarily, then slipped from my hand. Ashes sprayed in all directions like swirling clouds, and it crashed to the deck. I fumbled through the soot, kicked the barbecue accidentally, missed it with my hands and followed it helplessly across the deck as it banged and clattered toward the edge. In desperation, I lost my temper and pushed it onto the lawn. There it finally thumped to a stop.

When I entered the house, dusting ashes from my clothes, there was pandemonium in the rear hall. The coyotes were at the door trying to escape. Rogue was scratching wildly at the bottom, eyes wide with

Play continued at an accelerated pace. Shasta was the more aggressive and was always on top. Often Rogue would squeal, apparently with pain, but when we checked we could see he was not being bitten.

excitement, and Shasta was leaping toward the top, panting hard with every jump. As she leaped, one paw kicked the hall light switch, turning the light on, and as she came down her paw hit the switch again, turning the light off. The bulb pulsed like lights at a rock-music festival increasing the coyotes' terror. I grabbed Rogue and Peggy took Shasta and we tried to calm them, talking softly and rubbing their backs. It took more than one hour to calm them enough to lead them from the hall, and it was another hour before we could persuade them to eat.

The coyotes were so active that one pair often seemed like a pack, and as they raced around us in noisy circles one night Peggy suggested, "We might get better results with one animal."

"One would be easier to train, and the house would be much quieter," I admitted.

Several people had asked for our coyotes. A motion-picture producer in Hollywood offered to take the male. His firm operated an animal refuge in Washington. Rogue could live there safe and well cared for and would be used in occasional motion pictures. Another friend had a hunting preserve in northern California. He was one of a few ranchers to consider wild animals important to ecology; coyotes were protected on his land, and the animal we set free there could run naturally and safe as long as it lived.

"In the beginning we did want only one coyote," I said. "But which one do we keep? Which do we send away?"

Shasta was the more adventurous. She was the thief, leaped higher, explored more and caused the greater trouble. Yet aggressiveness made her appealing. She was a leader, and we loved her. Sometimes Rogue seemed backward. Not particularly brave, he was gentler and easier to handle, never in trouble and never a thief. We loved him for the combination of traits. It would be difficult to know which one to send away.

"If we separated them, both coyotes would be lonely," Peggy said finally.

"I'd miss it, too," I added.

That ended our discussion. We kept both coyotes. Shasta and Rogue raced happily around us oblivious of our talk, the noise level held loud and high and we never regretted our decision. If our coyotes could learn to adjust to civilization, we could learn to adjust to them.

Shasta howling. They seem to enjoy howling and do it often after a little urging from us.

Chapter Three

IT WAS NOW LATE FALL. Shasta and Rogue were eight months old, nearly full grown, and their summer pelage had given way to a thick winter fur that made them seem larger than they truly were. They were beginning to have the markings of adults—basically tones of light brown, although Shasta's fur was more reddish than that of the animals we saw in zoos and photographs. They had black on the tips of their tails and in round spots on their knees, as if they had been kneeling in soot. A ridge of lighter-colored hair extended along their muzzles and served two functions, according to books we read. Cheek nibbling is a common practice with many wolves and coyotes, although neither of ours did this, and the lighter hair supposedly focuses attention on the areas generally bitten. In addition, some animal behaviorists believe the hair contrasts with the darker lips so that visual signals, such as the baring of teeth in anger, are more clearly seen.

It was obvious our animals were maturing, and if they were growing, so were we in terms of knowledge. Several things became suddenly clear to us. The first was that our coyotes could communicate a range of complex ideas by sight, sound and touch.

Their tails were indicators of health and attitudes—that is, were barometers of the way they felt. When the tails were held high, they were happy; when the tails were curled between their legs, the animals were frightened or submissive and when they ran, their tails followed gracefully like flowing scarves.

A sign of affection between coyotes. Though it looks fierce, they bite very gently. Rogue is doing the biting in this shot.

Sounds had other meanings. Spontaneous howls indicated joy or boredom, and I could recognize at least five variations—some long and melodious and others short and nervous. They also gave several kinds of yips. Some indicated pleasure; others offered information and still others, short and high-pitched, always preceded a series of howls. Whines were mostly conversational, soft and intimate.

Touch, normally centered about the face, was the most explicit communication of all. When one coyote took the other's muzzle gently by the mouth, the action expressed affection. They made a similar statement of tenderness when they held our hands in their mouths. Directions were given by poking or pointing with the nose.

A scent gland near the tail offered still another form of communication. The odor was as individual as fingerprints and was used for identification. When Shasta and Rogue were frightened they also exuded the unmistakable musky odor, although we could not detect it at other times. It was not unpleasant and was somewhat like the sweat of humans.

Sometimes communication combined several senses. One night Rogue relaxed on the living-room floor as Shasta explored the back hall. Suddenly she trotted to him, put her nose beneath his muzzle and jerked her head toward the back door. When he did not respond, she repeated the gesture, adding a soft, pleading whine. Rogue got up and followed behind her. She stopped near the door and pointed to the floor. Shasta had discovered a mouse hole she wanted to share. Rogue joined his sister, sniffing happily.

The second thing we discovered was that our coyotes trusted and needed us more than we had suspected. We believed that if turned loose they would run away, at least for a day or two; but we were wrong— as two incidents proved.

The first came unexpectedly as we returned late from fishing. Peggy and Erik were in the house cleaning our catch and I was unpacking the car. It was dark, with barely enough moonlight to help me make my way without stumbling. I assumed the coyotes were safely in their

Our coyotes trusted and needed us more than we suspected.

Erik feeds a cookie to Shasta.

Shasta would leap to the fireplace to eat cookies in peace; Rogue cannot jump and does not like heights.

Nearly one year old, Rogue with his favorite toy, a plastic bowl well chewed.

run and scarcely saw the animal that moved in the brush at the edge of the highway. Only a rustling there caught my attention, and I watched curiously as the leaves moved unnaturally against the wind. When an animal wriggled closer, I was startled to discover it was Shasta. She was wet and muddy and had obviously been free for several hours. She was happy to see me and licked my face as I carried her into the house.

Erik and I raced to the run. The gate had been ripped from its hinges, and Rogue was missing. A ring of weak light from the porch spread across the ground, ending at the empty run, too dim to be of help with our search. I called Rogue's name. When there was no answer from the darkness, I whistled. Could he have run away? It was possible, but I couldn't believe he would be far from his sister, since the two were inseparable. Erik and I moved slowly through the tall grass. At first there was no sign. Then I thought I saw an outline of something to my left, but in the darkness I could not be certain—until I realized Rogue was there, statue-still. When Erik tried to catch him, the coyote circled nervously out of reach. Then Erik called his name, and Rogue rolled over in a gesture of submission. When Erik carried him in his arms, he found the animal was trembling. The experience of freedom had been too much for him.

In the house we petted them, calmed them, gave them ice cream and discussed the incident. Erik's theory seemed the most plausible. He believed teenagers hiking on the road had seen the coyotes and thought it would be sport to release them. Since they could not tell we were gone they had worked fast, tearing the gate apart to open the run. The next morning I replaced it with a heavy door we could lock.

The second example of trust came a few days later. Our older son, Malcolm, phoned to tell us he had become engaged to Julie Russell, a girl he had met at college, and we were delighted. We invited them to our home for a vacation. When they arrived a week later the coyotes nuzzled them warmly, and when Malcolm tried to hold Julie's hand Rogue pressed between them for attention. We had never seen the coyotes accept new people as quickly.

"If you will take them for a walk, I'll take some photos," I suggested. "It will be easy. They trust you."

The two agreed and took the coyotes to the Toadtown Canal, part of a hydroelectric system that transports water to a small lake two miles below our home. A trail follows the cement-lined ditch. At our home it is rimmed on one side with tall pines and on the other by a steep bluff, but below it abruptly crosses a deep, eroded chasm and the only way over is on a narrow plank. A drop of thirty feet makes the walk across like a tightrope performance, and it can be unnerving if you look down.

The first time Peggy and I had walked the coyotes on the canal, Shasta had eagerly crossed the board, but Rogue, after two tentative tries, had pulled back. I had carried him, and then we crossed often in this way. Shasta was always first. She waited for us on the bank, and when I put Rogue down she danced around him with obvious superiority.

One day Rogue surprised me by insisting on walking. He made it and from that time always crossed on foot and seemed proud when

Peggy and Shasta crossing the canal bridge, from which Rogue fell.

Shasta left him alone. But he always considered the trip dangerous and unnecessary, scratching his way over with his body low, arched and tense. He tugged hard at the leash to get the trip over with as quickly as possible.

This time I followed Julie and Malcolm with several cameras. We walked fast, but at the chasm Malcolm stopped, asking me to take Rogue. "I don't think Rogue trusts me that much," he explained.

I exchanged my cameras for the leash and started over. Rogue pulled hard and seemed unusually nervous. Halfway across he missed his footing, teetered, almost regained his balance, then tumbled end over end into space. I dropped to my knees quickly to ease the pull on his neck as he swung helplessly at the end of the chain. I could hear him gasping frantically for breath.

Heavy timbers, used to brace the sides of the canal, jutted outward five feet below me. There was one close to Rogue, and I swung him toward it. His rear feet caught the wood and held, and I lowered the leash slowly until his front feet were resting on another timber. He stood still, breathing easier but frozen with fear, his tail curled between his legs. I was upside down, leaning far over the plank, and I arched myself blindly over the edge to find a footing on a timber beside him. I did not dare to drop the leash, for it was far to the ground and if Rogue fell he would be injured. The leash was my only control, yet I did not know how he would react.

He was shaking, and I could smell the musky odor of fear about him. I reached a hand beneath his body, and for a moment he seemed terrified enough to bite. If he did, we would both fall. My arms circled below him cautiously, and he tensed; then I could feel him relax, and I knew he trusted me. I lifted him and brought him close, then timber by timber inched our way to the bank.

I lowered Rogue to the ground, and Shasta came racing to us, her tail wagging happily. Outwardly she seemed anxious and concerned, but her mouth—curled in what could only be a mocking smile—gave the lie to that thought. She was laughing at Rogue for his clumsiness. He took one look and flung himself at his sister with rage. He was obviously embarrassed and had to be growling, "Shut up!"

On the walk home Rogue tried to keep distance between himself

Shasta enjoyed ice cubes and begged them from Peggy when she opened the refrigerator.

and the rest of us, but Shasta circled continuously, grinning wickedly. She was goading him. Suddenly he lost his temper and nipped savagely at her flanks. She squealed, danced away and then kept her distance. If she understood communication at all, she understood Rogue's meaning very well.

Chapter Four

THE IMPULSE TO ESTABLISH boundaries is deep and strong in every species from grasshoppers to gorillas; even creatures that fly need a place to return to, to live, gather food and raise young. Animal behaviorists call it a "territorial instinct," and the intuitive drive motivates the animal in its need to establish a territory and to protect from competition all that is inside. A well-policed area is essential: it guarantees food, security and survival.

When food is plentiful, a coyote's real estate may cover no more than five or ten square miles, although in winter, or in areas with less food, an animal may range twice that distance. Whatever the actual mileage, a coyote knows his territory intimately, its trails, stalking areas, protective cover, sunny slopes, watering holes and sleeping places. When he mates, he stakes out two homesites—a den when the pups are young and a rendezvous site when they are older.

I knew Shasta and Rogue were developing these basic instincts, but I understood neither their depth nor their importance. In retrospect it seems strange that the signals, as obvious as they were, could have become confused in my mind, but the events of January were unusually strange, and I made at least two mistakes.

At that time Elizabeth was often in the house when the coyotes came for their meals. Rogue ignored her, but Shasta came running, wriggling happily as she had done when she was a puppy. She often bit

The wood basket became a favorite sleeping place for Shasta, and Rogue looked on with a certain amount of envy.

Shasta with Elizabeth, our ancient English bull.

Elizabeth's muzzle in gentle affection, and the bulldog, short-tempered as only old ladies can be, would tolerate the attention for a few moments, then rush awkwardly at the coyote, growling with annoyance. Shasta would easily avoid the onslaught, dancing to one side or the other in good humor as she scurried off to dinner. My first mistake was to believe the relationship could continue indefinitely.

January was also the beginning of Shasta's oestrous cycle. Coyotes rarely conceive during their first year, and I was not particularly concerned since she would not breed. I failed to realize that the first cycle could signal the changes that come with maturity, and my second mistake was to disregard its real importance.

The events may have begun the night we returned from shopping and Elizabeth did not meet us in the drive, as she generally did. It was dark when I parked and called her name and there was no answer. Even as I began to unload groceries I had an uneasy feeling something had happened, and the feeling was confirmed minutes later when a friend stopped his pickup on the road above me. He called down, "I saw your dog lying beside the highway. I think she was hit."

Elizabeth, old, deaf and nearly blind, had been with us ten years. We had gotten her as a puppy, and she was like a close relative or an old friend. I pulled a flashlight from the car and checked the edge of the highway. The story was there: a patch of blood on the asphalt—she had walked onto the road neither seeing nor hearing the car and the driver had raced off, perhaps without knowing what he had done. She was not there, and that, at least, meant she could be alive.

I quickly checked the places she used most and found her lying beneath the house in a low, difficult-to-reach place. I called her name and she rose unsteadily, dragging her right front leg. Her eyes were glazed, and in the glare of the flashlight's rays I could see blood dripping from the corners of her mouth. I coaxed her to me and, when she came, carried her gently to the car.

In town, the veterinarian examined her thoroughly. Aside from a fractured shoulder, her most serious injuries were chipped teeth and a cut tongue. He smiled reassuringly. The damage was not as serious as it seemed. She could come home in one week and would recover quickly.

Shasta missed the bulldog and each night searched for her in the rooms of our home. As the days passed, we speculated on what would happen when the two met. At the end of the week, we brought Elizabeth home. Her right leg was taped to her body, she could barely walk and I laid her in the living room beside a blazing fire.

Peggy let the coyotes into the house and we stood back to watch the reunion. Shasta raced to the center of the room, suddenly realized Elizabeth was there and whirled. Before I knew what was to follow she leaped, fangs bared, lips curled menacingly above her teeth, hackles raised on her back. I raced toward Elizabeth, who did not realize what was happening, and reached her as the coyote struck. Elizabeth snorted in pain and surprise, and I grabbed Shasta's collar, lifting her off the floor. She dangled helplessly beside me, clawing at the air. Rogue was only mildly interested, and Erik calmed him. Peggy lifted Elizabeth and carried her from the house, staggering under the weight. Then I released Shasta, and suddenly and surprisingly, she became calm.

It was a mystery. Her actions were puzzling. There was no reason for her hostility. A week before, the two had been friends, yet now Shasta wanted to attack the bulldog. Why? What had happened? Erik suggested that the dog's injuries, perhaps even the bandages and hospital odor, had caused it. Peggy thought it was the oestrous cycle. She said Shasta was jealous of other females.

The injury theory seemed the more plausible, since Elizabeth's accident was the most obvious change. I could see it and Shasta could, and to support that theory I even recalled that Dr. Durwood Allen, a famous biologist who studied Canadian wolves, had reported that wolves would sometimes kill injured pack members. But that night none of us truly knew what had caused Shasta's actions. I decided to restage the reunion. It was possible that only the suddenness of their meeting had triggered Shasta's moves. A second reunion might come off better.

Peggy let the coyotes into the house the next evening as I stood beside Elizabeth. Shasta ran happily to the center of the living room, saw Elizabeth and turned to attack. I caught her by the collar again, but this time she was most angry—snarling, growling and twisting in an attempt to bite me. I immobilized her by lifting hard. Peggy put the bulldog into the garage, and I released Shasta before I discovered the kitchen door was open. The coyote made the same discovery and raced toward it to renew the battle. We reached the door together, and I slammed it hard, pinning the coyote against the jamb, half outside, half in. Wriggling and scratching, she attempted to squirm free, but I held her. Reaching one hand below her, I suddenly released the door and flipped her end over end into the kitchen. While she was struggling to regain footing, I closed the door. Again she surprisingly relaxed, as if she had forgotten the incident. The contrast in emotions was strange, and I could find no ready explanation.

We kept the animals separated. Elizabeth slept in the house until it was time for the coyotes to eat and play with us, then was put into the garage. The routine worked well until she recovered enough to run free. Then we established a new pattern: we let her run as she wished until it was time to exercise the coyotes; at that time she was locked in the house. The plan involved a shuffling of animals twice daily, but peace was worth the effort. The plan worked until Elizabeth appeared on the lawn one day as we were walking the coyotes. We had forgotten to lock the house. Shasta and Rogue strained against their leashes to reach her.

"Back, Elizabeth go back!" I commanded, but the dog continued to move toward us with a plodding, rolling gait. She did not hear me and kept moving forward like a brindle tank without realizing the impending danger. Shasta struggled nervously against her leash, then leaped. I tightened the chain so that she could not harm the bulldog, but Shasta dropped short of the mark voluntarily. Instead of pressing the attack she rolled over, twisting and wriggling submissively.

The sudden reversal of her attitude startled me. What had happened now? Erik's theory, which had seemed so plausible a week ago, was falling apart. There had to be another explanation. I discovered it one week later.

A friend brought a giant male dog, half boxer and half Great Dane. The animal towered above the coyotes, who watched intently from their run. Shasta's eyes were wide with obvious, pointed interest. She bowed her head coyly and pawed the air submissively, and the dog trotted to the run to touch her nose. Without warning, Rogue bristled, hurtling himself at the intruder, his body thundering against the wire that enclosed the run. With hackles raised, he threw himself again and again against the wire, and it bulged outward from the force of his anger. In contrast, Shasta still wriggled a coy welcome beside him. Rogue suddenly whirled, nipped her flank angrily, sent her squealing and turned to attack the dog again. When we pulled the giant animal from the run, Rogue calmed immediately.

I knew then Rogue's actions were similar to his sister's. He was not really angry. He did not really want to kill or even harm the dog. The animal was an intruder and Rogue wanted to drive him off. I understood his motives and suddenly realized that they explained the many things we had witnessed that month. Our coyotes had developed strong territorial instincts. Competition was not welcome.

Peggy had been right, or close to it. Elizabeth's injuries had had nothing to do with Shasta's actions, although the accident, and the fact

When the boxer came for a visit, Rogue took exception to him immediately,
but Shasta liked the tall gent.

Shasta on the couch, Rogue on the floor. Their basic signals—between themselves and to others—were sometimes hard for us to understand.

that it kept the bulldog from the house for one week, may have accelerated the change. The explanation was simpler: with her first oestrous cycle, Shasta had grown up. She considered the house her territory and wanted no other animals in it. The situation had been reversed in the yard. She considered that area Elizabeth's and had rolled over to prove she did not want to argue over ownership. As I looked at our coyotes, now at peace in their run, I realized for the first time how strong their basic instincts must be.

Chapter Five

WE GAVE THE COYOTES heaping bowls of ice cream for their birthday, and their tongues darted over the melting richness like bright pink arrows. Rogue finished first, nosed Shasta's dish for more, then trotted to the couch where I sat reading. He pushed into my lap to be petted, and Shasta followed, squeezing between us. In the year they had been with us, the coyotes had become relaxed, friendly and at ease. They were less like playful pups and more like adults, and their calmer attitudes pleased us.

From the beginning we tried to look at situations from a coyote's point of view. We knew it was important to understand basic needs in their terms, and if we succeeded it was because we often accepted their conduct as normal even when it differed from ours. We knew it was the way to gain their trust.

As a consequence we began to see them as individuals. Rogue was placid, easygoing, the more conservative, the less humorous and a little like the Cowardly Lion. He would remain calm in most situations and was always deadpan and serious. Shasta was more active, more nervous, more intelligent. She laughed and smiled, was curious, shy and explosive, yet was the one we trusted more. If either coyote lost its temper, we felt Rogue would give less warning.

Walks became an essential part of their routine. The jaunts gave the coyotes a sense of freedom and time away from the run. At first we let

On their first birthday we gave them their first sample of ice cream. It was a hit, and after finishing theirs, they turned to Erik, insisting he share his with them.

them race free, but they ranged farther and farther until it was difficult to call them back, and in the end we walked with leashes.

Part of each walk was spent racing along the canal trail as Shasta and Rogue tugged at their chains, urging greater speed. Peggy and I ran until our lungs were ready to burst; then we made them stop. Another part of each walk was spent at a snail's pace as the animals sniffed and inspected the ground. They had checked both sides of the trail many times, yet on each walk they zigzagged and circled until it seemed as if we would never finish. On still other occasions they would pull us aside to some shaded area where the earth was soft, and we waited as they sniffed and scratched and dug huge holes. Often we were hunkered beneath a low tree, at chain's length, in an area where we could barely follow. Sometimes we walked more than three miles.

Their noses were extremely sensitive, and although we could not know it, snakes and lizards apparently have a distinctive odor. The coyotes could find them even at a run. They would whirl in their tracks, sniff the ground like bird dogs, then leap before we could pull back on the leashes. They usually caught game if it was within reach, although this was not often. I tried to discourage them from keeping or killing the animals they found, but it was difficult. They could not hunt well with us in tow, success was uncommon and because of the combination, the animals they caught were highly prized. When I realized that making them release game would eventually mean a confrontation with a snarling coyote who disagreed with my thinking, I relented. Common sense seemed the better part of valor, and Peggy and I would wait until the coyotes tired of their play.

I did not deliberately seek to disprove the prediction of the "experts" that our coyotes would turn on us by the time they were one year old, but I instinctively knew they were wrong and had an opportunity to prove my point that spring. Rogue had lost much of the hair on his chest. It came off suddenly, and an area between his front legs was as bald as the day he was born. He had to be taken to a veterinarian for an examination.

Every outing began at a snail's pace while the coyotes meticulously sniffed and inspected the ground.

Peggy walks with Rogue in a field near our home.

"While he's there, try to get his vaccinations," Peggy suggested.

People who knew animals told us it would be impossible to get any wild animal into a doctor's office and even harder to give one shots. "A strange room with strange odors and equipment will panic any animal. You'll have to bring the doctor to your house," one game warden warned. But Peggy and I were certain Rogue would do exactly as we wanted. Dr. Evers was willing to try, and the next afternoon I took the coyote to his office. Instead of leading Rogue by the leash, I carried him to the metal examining table as the nurse stood uneasily against the wall, out of danger yet apprehensive. Rogue did not fight and stood calmly as Dr. Evers cautiously examined his furless chest.

"Labels make cheap dog foods sound as nutritious as the expensive brands," Evers explained, rubbing the clear area on Rogue's chest, "but they are not. Rogue's problem is simple: he's not getting the right nourishment. If you switch to a better brand of food, the problem will dis-

56

appear." Then he prepared syringes with distemper and hepatitis vaccine. Rogue watched with growing interest and stirred uneasily. The doctor's nurse moved farther back, and I began to wonder if we could do it.

I stroked and petted the coyote, shielding his head as the doctor gave the first shot. Rogue flinched, then calmed immediately when I spoke to him, and when the first vaccination was completed without an angry reaction, Evers grabbed the second.

"I wasn't certain we could get away with it," Evers said when he had finished. "Few domestic dogs will take two shots without some argument. I've never seen a wild animal as gentle. Rogue trusts you completely." I drove home glowing with pride as Rogue lay contented and relaxed beside me. We changed his food that night, and within a week the fur returned.

As certain as we were of our coyotes, we were also realists and knew that no wild animal can ever be completely trusted. Instinctive reactions show under stress, and either coyote could bite us any time it felt threatened or insecure. Because of this possibility, I rejected as too dangerous

Rogue and Peggy. Outdoors the coyotes were alert to every sound and movement.

the "bat game" when Erik suggested it. But he persisted, and one night I reluctantly gave in. Erik wrapped himself in a sheet and chased both coyotes around the room, swooping low behind them, the sheet billowing like giant wings. The coyotes scurried past us, racing between the legs of tables and chairs. Erik caught Shasta, wrapped her in the sheet and turned her over as she kicked and clawed. Then he let her go. That was the game.

Rogue hated it. After the first round he sought sanctuary beneath the coffee table, where he tried to be quiet and invisible, but Shasta pawed and tugged at the sheet until Erik agreed to play again. The two raced around the room in tightening circles, and Erik whipped the sheet over her. She rolled on her back like a giant snowball, kicking and clawing until Erik let her go. The "bat game" became a favorite, and Shasta often asked Erik to play. Within a few days, she too was circling with her own wings—a short piece of sheet held in her mouth. It billowed behind her as Erik's flowed behind him.

Shasta seemed to like the roughness and speed of the game, and no matter how strenuous the play, she never became frightened and never growled. Rogue always watched from the safety of the coffee table, sometimes looking concerned for his sister and sometimes looking as if he wanted to join the fun.

There were times that spring when the coyotes seemed to devise their own jokes. One afternoon Peggy bought a call, a device she blew to produce sounds the manufacturer said would draw a variety of animals. Her plan was to call rabbits and squirrels so that I could take pictures, but when we heard the noises she produced, neither Erik nor I believed the plan would work. Our attitude angered Peggy.

She stomped up the hill behind our home to hide in the brush, and for more than one hour we could hear her honking and twittering. She tried high, shrill shrieks and low, puffing sounds, but neither interested as much as a butterfly. Finally, Erik could stand the tension no longer and hiked to her hiding place.

He said, "You'd better quit."

"Why?" she demanded indignantly.

"Because it sounds like only one thing—an old lady blowing through a chunk of wood. Who'll believe that?" Erik shrieked with laughter.

Peggy shook the call under his nose. "You're dead wrong. I'll bet one dollar a wild animal answers the next time I blow."

She gave a loud blast that squealed and squeaked higher than any sound she had made before, and there was silence for several moments. Then her call was answered—by a loud, hearty howl from the coyotes.

Erik doubled with laughter and gave her a dollar.

Even as they were growing older, the coyotes still liked to play in the manner of puppies, but they kept mostly to themselves, and neither seemed interested in our cat, Russell. On rare occasions Rogue seemed willing to be friends and made halfhearted lunges as if to invite some reaction, but each time he was rebuffed as the cat stalked to another part of the room. Rogue gave up, and Russell usually leaped to the top of a six-foot partition that separated the living room from the kitchen. From its safety he would watch the coyotes with cold, expressionless eyes.

One night, Russell lay asleep on the kitchen counter. His tail hung limply over the edge and twitched occasionally. Neither of us saw him when we let the coyotes through the back door, and he slept peace-

At three months, Shasta chases Rogue across our cat Russell's favorite chair. The coyotes and the cat ignore each other—most of the time.

fully. Rogue raced down the hall toward his dinner, with Shasta just inches behind, and in the center of the room he suddenly swerved off course. Before we knew what he had in mind, Rogue clamped his mouth around the twitching tail and jerked.

Russell tumbled end over end, bounced off Rogue's head and sprawled on the floor, dazed and furious. Rogue seemed confused, as if he could not associate the tail with the cat that had followed. The two animals stared at each other; then Russell regained his composure and leaped away, clawing an escape route up one of the round posts that support the living-room ceiling. He sat on a perch at the top, fifteen feet above the floor, angry and indignant, hurling a barrage of hisses and howls at the coyotes. He would not come down even after we put the coyotes out for the night, and it was only after I went to bed, well after midnight, that I heard him sliding warily to the floor. If the experience taught Russell anything, it was caution. For weeks afterward, he jumped to his feet each time we opened and closed the door.

Chapter Six

I HAVE NOT TRIED to catalog or count the many stories about coyotes. There must be thousands, covering areas from Canada to Mexico and time from the Aztecs to the present, and if there is a difference between the tales it is this: red men praised the coyote, while the only stories white men tell are those which perpetuate an image of cowardice and deceit, and neither is a coyote trait. As a rule, the more recent the story the less likely it is to be true. This generation does not understand coyotes.

One day I showed Shasta and Rogue to a neighbor because I thought he would appreciate their qualities. The man liked wild animals and had photographed many, yet as we moved away from the run he looked at me questioningly.

"Why them"—he paused to search for the right word—"varmints?"

The fellow was just one of many who considered our coyotes worthless, useless animals. Others seemed to react as one might to snakes or earthworms, with an unreasoning mixture of fear and revulsion, and several people who had obviously never been closer than zoo-length to a coyote told us graphically how the animals reacted to children and pets. All of the stories were gory, bloody tales that nearly turned my stomach.

One midnight a couple awoke me by pounding on the door, and as I stood on the porch with the winter cold flooding around my pajamas, the man insisted Shasta and Rogue had to be shot because they would become uncontrollable. "They're a threat to all of us," he said. I slammed the door in the middle of his tirade.

A neighbor said, "Keep your distance during meals. Even a tame coyote will tear off an arm over food." Another maintained, "Coyotes are used to eating fur. You've got to give yours an occasional hide or they'll die." A third warned, "They'll become vicious once they smell blood."

None of these predictions checked with the things we were discovering. Shasta and Rogue eat canned dog food and do not like raw meat, yet consider cooked beef and chicken a treat. We can move their pans even as they are eating; they are neither angry nor uneasy and continue to feed, carefully avoiding our fingers. We've never given them hides and do not intend to. And once I cut a finger. Shouting in outrage, I clutched my injured hand, and Rogue trotted over to see what the noise was about. He seemed to believe I was hiding food and insisted on inspecting my hand. He discovered the blood welling up from the cut, sniffed it with little interest and walked away.

Contrary to the old saw, truth is often less exciting than fiction, and the truth about coyotes is this: coyotes are carnivores—as are dogs, cats and swallows hunting flies in the evening shadows. Coyotes are descended from the creodont, a prehistoric progenitor of the bear, cat, dog, raccoon and seal. One ten-million-year-old ancestor was twelve and one-half feet long and six feet tall. Another, a smaller, doglike hunter called *Tomarctus*, was a common ancestor to dogs, jackals and wolves. Coyotes sensibly avoid fights, because they know that to fight is to risk one's life. But when a battle is necessary, coyotes can fight with a skill and endurance few animals can equal. Coyotes have successfully defended their dens against many killers—bears, eagles, mountain lions and wolves. Coyotes often win against unbelievable odds. Coyotes are intelligent. Coyotes are curious. Coyotes are fast. Coyotes are America's smallest native wolf.

Do not misunderstand me. Every coyote has a weakness, a vulnerability, an Achilles' heel. As children love candy and as cats love catnip, coyotes are hooked on leather. From the youngest to the oldest, all members of the species have an insatiable appetite for it, and even the smallest, worn and torn piece draws them as a magnet draws iron. A coyote that can still be counted alive will do anything for it. In the days of covered wagons, coyotes crept into camp under cover of darkness to steal only one thing—harness; and we discovered that that impulse is still very much alive.

I left a pair of leather work gloves in the living room and Shasta found them, and by the time I saw her there was little reason to argue about questions of ownership. Half of one glove was gone, and the part that remained was being deftly separated finger by finger. When Rogue appeared she sent him scurrying with snarls, and I could tell she had a similar warning for me. I knew that if I tried to interfere, Shasta might be forced to decide between friendship and leather, and I didn't want to force that issue. I sat down, and Shasta kept her prize all evening, occasionally tearing off small tidbits and keeping the remains under firm control. She carefully hid the pieces in the hall, and we put her out for the night.

We had forgotten the incident by the next night and were instead more concerned with Rogue, who had suddenly become lame. When he stood, he would lift one paw and then another as if the pads were tender, and when he walked he moved as if in great pain. We checked his feet, but could find no sign of trouble—neither cuts nor swelling. Now he lay panting on a chair, in an unhappy, dark humor, and when Shasta came to him with sympathetic whimpers he growled grumpily.

Shasta circled the chair from a respectful distance as if puzzled, then

Shasta steals a work glove.

Julie and Malcolm harmonize with Shasta.

trotted to the hall. She returned in a few minutes with the torn remains of her glove and laid them on the chair beside her brother. We never discovered the cause of his illness, but it was evident her gift helped: Rogue was well by morning. If the incident makes any point, it is not that coyotes are anthropomorphic, as some film makers claim, but simply that wild animals have a range of feelings and responses that we rarely take time to understand.

Some writers say coyotes habitually eat anything and document their claims with a list of the contents of the stomachs of captured coyotes. It generally includes everything from fountain pens to paper plates. Hungry ones will scavenge, but given a chance a wild coyote prefers fresh food, generally rabbits and rodents, and if ours are any barometer, captive ones develop a sure sense of good taste and quality.

The two like cookies—preferring vanilla and chocolate, ignoring caramel and lemon. We kept a supply of inexpensive cookies on hand to use as rewards, and when either animal took something we wanted to retrieve or when we needed to lead them from one place to another or to divert their attention, cookies were our lure. The cheap kind worked well until Peggy made the mistake of baking almond-paste squares.

The coyotes watched with fascination as Peggy and Erik mixed a rich dough of almond, butter, eggs and cream and popped the squares into the oven. When they were ready, Shasta pushed to the head of the line, and Rogue was only inches behind. Reluctantly Erik gave one to each animal, and almond paste made an instant hit.

Both animals pressed close for seconds, but Erik decided to reserve the almond paste for himself and instead gave the coyotes the inexpensive cookies. Neither animal saw him make the substitution, and both grabbed the goodies he offered. They bit eagerly, then turned to do a surprised double take. With a look of disgust Shasta spat hers on the floor, and Rogue ate his as if in punishment.

We had heard stories of a coyote's love for fresh fruit, and that summer we had an opportunity to test the truth of it. Peggy planted strawberries near a flower bed we passed every time we walked the animals. While the bushes were maturing neither coyote showed any interest, but when the fruit began to develop they would pull us aside to check its progress. One day Rogue insisted on following a row. He pulled hard against his leash and would not quit, and I let him sniff the leaves. He nosed each plant carefully and finally stopped to pick one

Malcolm with Rogue, curious and yet wary.

berry. When I checked the plants he had passed, I found he had selected the only ripe fruit in the row. Later, when we let them pick berries, they took only the fully ripe ones, leaving the others for another day. They always enjoyed the feast and ate each berry with gusto.

A neighbor gave us three cantaloupes so large Peggy could store only two in the refrigerator, and the third was left on the kitchen counter. Shasta discovered it that night and stole the melon before we knew what she had in mind. In seconds she had it in her wide-open jaws, and Rogue, who had missed the action as we had, came to see what was happening. She managed a throaty growl and scurried to the couch, where she settled comfortably on the cushions. The melon rested between her paws, and she was so noticeably possessive we decided not to try to retrieve it as long as the melon remained intact. To be certain there was no mess, Peggy sat at one end of the couch.

Rogue immediately jumped beside her and leaned against Peggy's side in a rare display of affection. It was not his standard reaction, yet he seemed totally uninterested in everything else. Shasta watched him intently, her yellow eyes following him with suspicion. Peggy petted Rogue and he relaxed, his eyes almost closed. From appearances, at least, he was unconcerned about his sister's treasure.

Shasta sniffed the melon, rolled it across the cushions toward Rogue, then pulled it back with a warning snarl. She pushed the melon toward him again, goading him with her prize, but Rogue would not look at his sister. He relaxed and enjoyed the petting as her one-sided game continued. Eventually even I was convinced he was truly not interested.

Then Erik entered the room and Shasta turned her head momentarily to see what he was doing, and Rogue sprang to life. He leaped from Peggy's side, snatched the melon from between Shasta's paws and sped across the room, devouring the fruit in great gulps before any of us knew what had happened. He had planned the robbery and the plan had worked: he had gotten his prize without fighting, had fooled Peggy and me and had been so fast Shasta had forgotten to snarl. Actually, she seemed more astonished than angry.

Some of the stories people told were so patently preposterous they were fun to hear. To me the most fascinating of these are about a coyote's magical eyes, and one story I particularly like tells how a Mexi-

Julie running with Shasta.

Peggy holds a cookie and Shasta leaps for it.

can coyote catches chickens. The animal waits until dusk, when the birds are roosting, then creeps beneath the tree to stare intently at them until one is foolish enough to look down. Then, with the chicken's gaze locked in his, he walks in circles, never letting the fowl close its eyes or change its gaze. Eventually the bird becomes so dizzy it tumbles to the ground.

Another of my favorites concerns a coyote lucky enough to live beneath a date palm. Each year when the fruit begins to ripen the best dates are always out of reach, yet the animal has ways of getting the fruit he wants. He sits beneath a ripe bunch and moves his tail back and forth, and soon the dates begin to sway in rhythm with his tail. The story always ends in the same way. "You may not believe this," the narrator says, "but so help me, the dates fell directly into his mouth." Most of these tales originated in the Southwest. Some are more than a century old, and apparently some Indians still believe them. There are tribes below the border who insist a coyote can hypnotize a man and who say a coyote can shoot bolts of electricity from his eyes.

When I look into our coyotes' penetrating eyes I can almost believe the stories, and one night I thought I might actually see it happen. Russell was sitting on the top of the partition that separates the kitchen from the living room, and Rogue sat on the floor directly below, looking up at the cat. I was surprised to see Russell's head snap toward Rogue as their eyes locked in a duel of stares, and for several minutes neither animal moved.

I called softly to Peggy, "This is it, the coyote magic we've read about."

"You're mad," she replied, but I continued to watch as Rogue's dark eyes seemed to hold the cat fast. Russell's body rocked back and forth, and I expected to see him topple at any minute. Then, without warning, the cat stood up, stretched luxuriously and walked off, leaving Rogue bewildered and disappointed.

"Well, so much for the eyes," I said, petting him softly.

Chapter Seven

WHEN SCHOOL ENDED that summer, Erik enrolled in a camp near Gallup, New Mexico. It offered an opportunity for a variety of adventures—camping, hiking, exploring and even archaeology and herpetology—and he was eager to go. The only delay was transportation. An airplane necessitated two changes and an overnight stop, the bus was longer and even more complex and only the train, still running at that time, offered a direct routing. The line we would use, the Santa Fe, left from San Francisco, a hundred and fifty miles south of our home. Erik chose it.

We drove to San Francisco for a farewell party at a favorite restaurant and arrived at the station late. The cars were ready for boarding, lined up on an open track beside an old, yellowed waiting room and the afternoon sun sent long shadows against its wall. We swung quickly on board and found Erik's compartment. I piled his luggage in one corner while Peggy gave him a stack of dollar bills.

"When the gong sounds, go to the dining car. Order a complete meal and don't skimp," she insisted protectively. Erik nodded. This was his first train ride, and I suspected he was embarrassed by us, by a paucity of knowledge of what was expected of him and by a lack of confidence.

I remembered my first train ride and the embarrassment of it, and the day came back to me as I stood in the compartment. I was eight, returning from a vacation on my uncle's farm, seated beside a window on a upright purple velvet seat that prickled uncomfortably. My aunt had given me a box of pretzels, which were eaten ravenously, and my overwhelming memory of the remainder of the trip is water, tasting of tin, warm and pouring slowly from a tank near the door into triangular paper cups that held barely a mouthful. I thought I could understand the way Erik felt.

I told Peggy, "Don't worry. He's big enough to make it alone."

Then we were outside, the train was pulling away from the station and we waved eagerly. Erik answered from the window, a slight smile on his face. The train disappeared, and the crunch of our timetable began.

I had an assignment to photograph parts of the Southwest where coyotes figured prominently in early legends and had promised to meet Erik when his camp was finished seven weeks later. There was only one problem: if Peggy was to come, and we certainly wanted that, we could not leave our own coyotes behind. At best it was a mixed blessing. On one hand, many tourists carry pets, dogs or cats, but none share vacations with coyotes, and that realization gave me a feeling of cool one-upmanship; yet at a practical level, it would not be an easy trip. The coyotes could not have the freedom of household pets, and if they were to go they had much to learn.

The logistics were these: we had to teach the coyotes to travel, to ride calmly and easily; we had to be sure they received precautionary vaccinations and we had to outfit a vehicle that would keep them safe and secure. The combination was no small order and seven weeks no great amount of time.

The coyotes had not ridden since they were pups and needed re-training. On the first day neither animal wanted to get into the station wagon. We stuffed them unceremoniously through the door like fur pillows and sat with them for half an hour, the car stationary, its engine off, repeating the procedure for four days. On the fifth, when they were relatively calm, I started the engine. They leaped over each other like mad acrobats, eyes wide with a mixture of fear and surprise. Shasta circled as if the world had come to an end, and Rogue scratched for a way out. We repeated that phase of training several times, increasing the length of their stay in the car, and finally I put the vehicle in gear and inched along the drive. It was the end of the second week.

The third week began on the highway. Peggy sat in the rear as we

71

moved forward. Rogue quickly curled beside her with his head on her lap, but Shasta paced nervously. Although less excitable than when we began, she was not at ease and paused frequently to peek out the rear or to test the air through the partly opened windows. We repeated the drive every evening, and while Shasta eventually became accustomed to the car, she never trusted any part of our training program, rarely relaxing or sitting. She was most nervous when a car came from behind; the closer the vehicle, the more she paced, as if to outdistance it.

When the cars passed, I would try to find the driver's face in my mirror; I wanted to see the reaction when the fellow discovered he was staring into the cold yellow eyes of a coyote who didn't trust him and who hoped he would evaporate, disappear or turn in another direction. Few drivers saw Shasta, but those that did made my time worthwhile. Many did double takes, some had looks of complete disbelief and one drove past shaking his hands as if to tell me there was something very strange in the back of my car.

Less than three weeks remained, and now that the coyotes were used to the highway, speed and motion, I drove to a supermarket, where they sat in the car. The objective was to get them accustomed to being alone with strangers outside. In the beginning, even the most distant person disturbed Shasta; she would back into a corner, hissing violently. But Rogue seemed calm, and Shasta gradually relaxed. Yet one day, as I returned with my arms loaded with groceries, she eyed me suspiciously, and when I touched the car she recoiled, growling angrily.

"For God's sake, it's me!" I shouted. She swung her head, her mouth opened then closed, her tail wagged and as I sat down she seemed apologetic, smothering me with her wet tongue. We took them with us daily, and they were beginning to accept travel as a regular part of their lives. If the schedule continued to progress as smoothly, we might make it.

Erik's letters grew more exciting. He was on the move, camping in tents in the New Mexican backcountry, searching for Indian ruins and trapping snakes to be given to a zoo. While excavating near one ruin, his group discovered an eight-hundred-year-old coyote skull once used in religious ceremonies. That news heightened my interest to see the country where so many fascinating legends had begun, and I worked hard to complete our projects. Vaccinations were next on the list, and two weeks remained.

Archaeologist Dick Lang, from Erik's summer camp, with a coyote skull estimated to be eight hundred years old, recovered from Pueblo ruins and probably used in religious ceremonies. Indians considered that the wit and cunning of a coyote were transferred to the man who possessed the skull.

The coyotes had had preliminary vaccinations when they were pups, but needed more. We had been told it was a state law that wild animals transported into California, even those reentering, needed rabies protection. That meant our animals now needed two shots—a distemper booster and the rabies vaccination. Since they were most excitable together, I felt the process would go best if I took them to the doctor's office separately. Rogue was no problem; his shots were finished in a matter of minutes. I was tempted to believe Shasta could be handled as easily, although I knew she was more nervous and excitable. The next day I took her to the office and she surprised me by standing calmly on the examining table as Dr. Evers prepared the syringes.

I held her head in my arm so that she could neither turn nor see the doctor. He gave her the distemper booster, then readied the rabies injection, and suddenly Shasta whipped from my grasp to face him, mouth open, lips parted menacingly. She had caught a movement in a corner of her eye and was now aroused, snarling a mixture of fear and apprehension. The syringe stopped in midair as Dr. Evers hesitated, trying to decide what to do. I forced my arm into her mouth so that she could neither bite nor leap and carried her to the Jeep. She resented being tricked, blamed the doctor and cowered in one corner of the wagon, hissing with rage.

"We won't be able to get her into your office again today," I said.

"I could try to give the shot here," Evers offered, but as he touched the tailgate Shasta lunged at him, and it was obvious that if he moved again she would bite.

"We'll have to try tranquilizers," he said. "With one or two, you should be able to bring her to my office relaxed enough to handle."

The doctor seemed confident, but I wasn't as optimistic, since few animals can be as stubborn as coyotes. Once Shasta or Rogue decided against a thing there was no way to talk it into reversing the decision, and I was certain Shasta had decided Dr. Evers was not to be trusted. We went into Evers' office and he counted out a handful of white tablets, explaining the way in which they worked.

Victory! We're ready for our trip through the Southwest. Both coyotes had had their rabies shots, and I drove to the doctor's office to pick up the certificates I had been told we needed to get them back into the state. The picture shows me with Dr. Henry Evers and the coyotes in the camper we made for them.

Tranquilizers, he said, would calm Shasta without drugging her—an important distinction. Under their gentling influence she could retain knowledge, so that we might later bring her to his office without tranquilizing and without a violent reaction. On the other hand, drugs like barbiturates were unpredictable. Each animal is affected in a different way, and it is not always a good experience. Evers wanted to reserve barbiturates for an emergency. I wasn't certain that either medication would work, and for the first time since we had planned the trip, success seemed impossibly far away.

The next day I began tranquilizer tests and when one tablet had no effect doubled the dosage. Shasta slowly became groggy, as predicted, but was also short-tempered and nervous, not as predicted. The slightest sound upset her, and she whirled to face the source of each noise, growling with annoyance. It was as if she knew she was losing control and compensated for her diminishing faculties with exaggerated caution. In the wilderness the reaction would make sense, but in the run it only meant more tablets.

The next day I tried three, and she quickly became groggy. For the first time, Rogue seemed to sense a change. He pushed her and she staggered, yelping loudly. The hairs on Rogue's back were raised in anger, and he hit her again and again with his flanks like a football lineman battering his opposition, and when she fell he straddled her, glaring angrily into her eyes. A low growl was building in his throat.

I raced to the run, opened the door and petted Rogue—a potentially foolish move, since I had never seen him act this way and could not be certain he would not turn on me, but I had few options. The situation seemed to need direct action. In time he relaxed and Shasta raced to safety, then circled the run nervously and returned, demanding attention. Rogue turned on her a second time, not biting hard to draw blood, although his anger seemed authentic. I could not understand the situation. It was real yet unreal. Perhaps it was a game, since Shasta had returned to be bullied, but I did not trust the outcome and chained Rogue to a tree outside the run. When I returned him, two hours later, he sniffed Shasta once and walked away, and the mystery deepened. If the pills were not affecting Shasta, they were driving me crazy. Only a few days remained; we had to try barbiturates, even though they were a more dangerous drug. I prayed they would have a better effect.

Peggy walking Shasta at Bluewater Lake in New Mexico. We walked the animals daily to keep them happy and easier to handle.

Checking on the coyotes during the day—something we did often during the trip.

I received new tablets from Dr. Evers and began experimenting with dosages. Neither one nor one and one-half tablets had any effect. With two, Shasta became surprisingly affectionate. She wandered aimlessly from room to room, unsteady and uncertain, yet retaining enough control to resist Dr. Evers. While the drug seemed better than tranquilizers, a still greater dosage was required. I called the doctor for instructions.

"Perhaps I should come to your house," he offered. "Shasta will fight less in familiar surroundings. Give her three tablets before I arrive; that's twice the amount I give to any dog. She will be unconscious before I get there, but don't be alarmed."

I felt guilty and remorseful for the trick I was about to perpetrate, but I knew that if any animal could subvert accepted medical practices, obvert the norm and turn everything contrariwise, it would be a coyote. Only a coyote could reverse the pattern of drugs so that barbiturates produced euphoria, happiness and affection and tranquilizers uptight uncertainty. I gave Shasta three pills disguised in hamburger, and soon

Rogue at Bluewater Lake. He finds a tin can, a favorite toy, and plays with it.

she was drunk, uncertain, barely able to walk yet stubbornly refusing to succumb to the powerful pull of the drug. She was gamely on her feet when the doctor arrived, and as he sat amazed by her performance she weaved past, suspiciously sniffing at his leather bag.

"It's surprising. I didn't think any animal her size could resist that much barbiturate," Evers said.

Half an hour later she was still conscious, weaving aimlessly, stumbling and staggering but forcing herself to remain upright, in motion and conscious. Each time she passed Evers she "woofed" to let him know she was expecting a trick. She refused to give in. Her willpower was impressive.

Evers opened his leather bag, and Shasta almost fell into it as she came to investigate. He readied a syringe, and I bent over, picked up Shasta and held her in my arms. She did not resist, but looked at me wearily and dropped her head against my chest. Her eyes were almost closed. Dr. Evers moved toward her from one side, out of the range of her vision, and inserted the needle in her leg. She did not seem to feel the pressure of it.

I continued to hold her as the doctor repacked his equipment. Her eyes were closed, her head hung limply over my arm and yet, when Dr. Evers left, she opened one eye, fixed it unsteadily on him and managed a stern "grufff" that told him not to try anything. Then she was unconscious. I laid her on the couch, removed her collar and attached the shining new rabies tag Evers had left behind.

Chapter Eight

AFTER SIX HOURS on the road, with Peggy and me in the truck and Shasta and Rogue in the camper, we stopped in the high desert near Fallon, Nevada, and I erected the canvas-topped trailer. The last rays of sun sent long shafts of light across the sand, and the sage made weird, almost human shadows. The mountains were turning purple, blue and gray, and the sky was a rich red. Peggy began dinner on a small kerosene stove, and when I finished my job we ate beside the trailer as the coyotes dined beside us. Two days of travel remained before we joined Erik, and if they went as easily there would be no trouble.

But the first day was deceptive. On the second evening, when we arrived at the Lehman Caves National Monument, high on the eastern slopes of Wheeler Peak, we found the park full. The only unused site was near one corner of the campground, small, enclosed by trees and brush.

When the coyotes were let out, Rogue pulled to the end of his chain and shivered, looking apprehensively over his shoulder, and Shasta tugged violently until she gasped for breath. Rogue snarled when I tried to comfort him, and Shasta circled nervously so that I could neither touch nor corner her. Both refused attention and would not eat. Finally we carried them to the truck, and they calmed quickly.

A partial explanation of their behavior came when we compared this camp with the one at Fallon. Shrubbery rimmed the Lehman site

Our campsite in the desert near Fallon, Nevada.

like a green cover, and while the coyotes could not see other campers, they could hear and smell them. Danger could lurk behind every bush and in the coyote mind probably did. Shasta and Rogue were frightened by the things they couldn't see; in comparison, the site at Fallon had been safe because it was open and danger could be seen from a great distance.

The campground was our downfall, too. The dinner menu included hamburger patties and green beans, and Peggy began preparations after we locked the coyotes in the truck. A fire blazed merrily beneath a pot of water, yet the meal progressed slowly. "If it's going to take long, I'll make a drink," I said finally. "We deserve one."

We relaxed at the picnic table over bourbon, and the water in the pot simmered lazily, refusing to boil. Each time I checked it the coyotes rustled uneasily in the truck, and time seemed to drag. When I finished my drink and the water was still only lukewarm, I poured a second round. We continued to wait. The sun disappeared, the camp became dark and I lit a kerosene lantern.

"Surely we'll be able to eat soon," I said mixing a third drink. Finally we put the beans in a half-warm pot and placed hamburgers in a pan, and eventually things were ready. The meat was half cooked and the beans were raw, but it no longer mattered. The campground was weaving and swirling overhead, we were laughing at almost everything that happened and when we walked we bumped into tables and trees.

We were drunk—unintentionally, unexpectedly, suddenly and thoroughly drunk—and the explanation came over me like a wave: the camp was at nine thousand feet. The great elevation was the reason the water took so long to boil, the reason the meal was half cooked and the reason alcohol hit us so hard. Shasta whined softly, and still drunk enough to believe everything was hilarious, I shouted to her, "You think you've got troubles." I leaned against the bench laughing hysterically.

The next day was little better. In midafternoon we were in Utah, and I drove the truck through the scenic areas of the Cedar Breaks National Monument to make photographs. On the way out, I discovered an inviting, green meadow at the edge of federal land—empty, open and unused. It ran north and south, merging on my right with a gentle hill clustered with trees and extending across the highway on my left into a second field with a few stands of pines and firs. It was an ideal place to walk Shasta and Rogue, and I parked on a dirt road at one end of the field. The coyotes leaped out, eager to run. I put a camera and exposure meter around my neck, and we started into the field.

Peggy had Shasta on one leash and I had Rogue on the other. Scents in the grass excited them instantly, and they ran before us, noses to the ground, tails wagging happily. We raced a quarter of a mile at top speed until the terrain changed to marshy land with hummocks of tufted grass a few inches apart. Around each tuft I could see holes, and the cause of the coyotes' excitement became obvious. Dozens of voles, or meadow mice, leaped before us. The marsh was alive with them.

Voles are common throughout much of the United States—rodents about four inches long with short ears, moderate hair and tiny claws with thumblike projections on the hind feet. They eat grass, roots, seeds and bark and are as much at home in a farmer's field as in a mountain meadow. Many ranchers consider them destructive, unwanted pests. As I watched them scatter before us, I could understand why almost every predator from snakes and hawks to coyotes and wildcats preys on them. Utterly defenseless, the tiny rodents were certain food.

They ran in all directions like gray windup toys, and Rogue's head swiveled as he tried to keep track of them. Though he had never needed his hunting instincts before, the urge welled up strong in him now and he tensed, ready to leap. Shasta was beside him, mouth open, not quite believing what she saw.

Rogue pounced, and only the leash kept him from a catch. Even I had difficulty avoiding the animals, for mice were everywhere, almost like a moving carpet. Rogue pounced again and caught one in his mouth. He held it proudly by the loose fur on its back and shook his head. The animal rocked from side to side lifelessly, and the movement excited Rogue and he shook his head again, with more violence. The vole slipped from his mouth and cowered with fear beneath his paws. Rogue sniffed the grass but could find neither the animal nor its trail, and the mouse scooted to safety. Rogue was still searching for his prize when I petted him comfortingly.

"You're lucky to have us. You'd starve on your own," I said. Even though the vole's role was to provide food for larger animals, I was happy he had escaped. I did not want to see him killed.

We worked deeper into the marsh as the coyotes danced and leaped before us and the mice scattered almost as if it were a game. A dull clanging of bells, like those of cows, came faintly from the wooded slope on our right, and I stopped. We listened intently. Animals were coming to the meadow from somewhere behind the trees, and we moved leisurely east, away from the sound, sometimes walking, sometimes running.

But the ringing continued, insistent and louder, and I could see it came not from cows but from sheep. A herd of fifty or more was winding slowly toward the meadow like a white ribbon unrolling down the hill. In the rear was a sheepherder on a black horse.

"Let's get out of here; he could mean trouble!" Peggy shouted.

The line of sheep was heading directly toward us and would shortly intersect our route. We would have to continue away from them until we gained sufficient distance to cut across their flank. There was no reason to worry, but we walked faster, and although it was difficult to believe, the sheep seemed to be moving faster as well. I could plainly see the rider and four dogs, and the line of white animals seemed to be

Sheepmen are the enemy of coyotes, as we discovered in Utah. One threatened to kill the coyotes even though they were on leashes.

gaining distance on us. I knew sheep dogs are trained to protect flocks, and the last thing I wanted was for them to attack Shasta or Rogue.

Neither coyote seemed disturbed by the intrusion, and they still walked easily with us sniffing mouse holes as we went. We came to the edge of the marsh, the earth was hard again and we began to run, the camera and meter banging against my chest. Unbelievably, the line of sheep was still aimed at us and definitely closer. I could not believe we had been moving that slowly. We crossed the highway and circled north toward our truck. The altitude, about ten thousand feet, made breathing difficult, and I was gasping loudly.

Suddenly Rogue flattened against the ground, refusing to move. I didn't know why he had stopped but welcomed the rest and stood beside him panting. Perhaps we were being foolish to run, but the dogs bothered me. If they came to investigate, there could be a fight we would not be able to stop. Suddenly the sheep changed course.

"Good God! The herder is trying to run us down," I shouted. Peggy stared unbelievingly at the white line that was again aimed directly at us. We were no longer running to keep a safe distance but were running to avoid danger, chased by a man who obviously meant trouble. My mind sought a reason and there was no answer, yet the white line of animals loomed larger and closer. The situation had become serious.

I scooped Rogue into my arms. He did not resist, but his weight, almost forty pounds, tugged at my arms, and the bulk of the camera and light meter whipping against my chest added to my problems. I ran in earnest, sprinting as fast as I could, but I seemed to be racing on a tread-mill, and Peggy and Shasta quickly outdistanced me. The truck was still a quarter of a mile away, and the sheep were closer—only a few hundred feet to my left. I realized it would be impossible to reach safety.

Gasping for air, I stopped running and put Rogue on the ground. Peggy came back to stand beside me, and the four of us faced the ap-proaching sheep with our backs to a tall pine. They came undulating like a giant white worm and stopped less than fifty feet away. The herder, still in the rear, was flanked by dogs who watched with expres-sionless faces: three big males, a female nearly as large and a pup. They waited as if for a command to attack.

"Keep your dogs away," Peggy shouted.

The herder rode slowly to the front of the line. He sat on his horse, towering above us like John Wayne in a Western movie. He was an old man, and beneath his dirty Stetson the stubble of an unshaven white beard stood out against his weathered, tense face.

"What do you want?" I asked. "Let us past."

The man did not answer, but sat silently looking down as if in judgment. Shasta and Rogue pulled against their leashes, watching first the sheepherder and then his dogs. Neither coyote seemed afraid, even though the dogs moved restlessly. A full-chested male came to Shasta, stopping just beyond reach and she pulled against her leash. The pup ran to Rogue barking lustily, and Rogue tensed. The hackles on his back were raised and he lunged, brought up short by the chain. The pup, though it had not been touched, leaped back in surprise and ran to its mother, yelping. I expected its cries would trigger an attack, but the dogs remained motionless. In that moment I knew how it felt to be hunted. We were at bay as surely as a fox, a bear or a wildcat. Finally the old man spoke.

"Why you got coyotes?" he demanded.

That was it! Suddenly his motives were clear. It was the coyotes he was after. I knew sheepmen hated coyotes, and even though ours were on leashes this herder had chased us across the meadow to see why we were here.

"They're pets. I'm taking pictures" I waved the camera around my neck.

"You got no right. We killed all coyotes here years ago and we don't want none back."

"But we have every right. This is public land. We're doing no harm," I protested.

"I don't give a damn. I'll kill 'em."

"But they're harmless. They're on leashes," I protested.

"Don't matter. I'll kill 'em anyway," he said stubbornly.

"You won't touch these," I shouted, crouching close to Rogue. There was a rifle in a scabbard beside the old man's saddle, and if he was going to shoot he would have to aim at both of us. I didn't think he would try that. The herder watched me carefully.

"Then get out while you got a chance." His eyes were fixed with such hatred I knew he meant exactly what he said and our only choice was to do as he ordered. Any other move would risk Shasta's and Rogue's lives. I prayed the coyotes would come without resistance and that the dogs would remain under control. Cautiously I pulled on Rogue's leash, and he turned slowly, following me. Then Shasta came with Peggy and we were across the highway and at the truck. I opened the door, the coyotes jumped in and I locked it. The sheepherder came up the trail to make certain we were leaving.

I was shaking with a mixture of excitement, fear and anger as I drove down the highway. The image of things that might have happened raced through my mind. Had either the dogs or the coyotes shown fear or anger, the situation might have been different. An animal or even a human could have been injured. The old man must really have hated coyotes to risk so much.

The U.S. Park Service station at Duck Creek was ahead, and I turned the truck into the parking lot. There I talked with the ranger in charge, Foyer Olsen. He stood by our truck looking through the door at Shasta and Rogue as I explained the incident in detail. Olsen did not seem disturbed by the story, and weeks later I received a letter which dismissed the incident.

"I contacted Merril Thornton, herder for T. Randall Adams, and we discussed his threats," Ranger Olsen wrote. "After thinking over the incident Mr. Thornton expressed his regrets for acting as he did and for losing his temper. When I talked with you I mentioned the hate and distrust sheepmen have for coyotes and Mr. Thornton mentioned this. Since he is about 65 years old and has worked with livestock all of his life, I hope you will not judge him harshly."

Neither Peggy nor I judged the old man harshly, even though his actions could have had serious consequences. We had expected to find unreasoning prejudice in the sheep-raising states.

Chapter Nine

WE ARRIVED IN KANAB, Utah, at sunset; settled for space in a crowded mobile-home park because no public areas were available and signed in without mentioning our cargo. We were convinced that in Utah, at least, it was wise to keep friendly coyotes a secret.

As I erected the trailer, a dachshund who seemed to belong to a mobile home across the road discovered the scent of Shasta and Rogue and began barking in round after round of excited, high-pitched yelps as if coyotes were his private war. If the dog continued long, the manager would come to investigate and could ask us to leave. It was dark and too late to find another space, and since I did not relish camping beside the road, I ran toward the annoying animal waving my arms. He retreated reluctantly.

When the trailer was erected, Peggy and I went to bed. The evening was warm, and I relaxed in my sleeping bag without pajamas. It had been a long, disturbing day and I was drowsy, but as sleep pulled me closer the dachshund returned, barking a new round of challenges. I rolled out of bed, dressed, chased the animal again and calmed Shasta and Rogue. Then I undressed and closed my eyes—but at least hourly thereafter the sharp, high-pitched anxious barking of that dog pulled me from the edge of sleep and the pattern was the same: out of bed, dress, chase the dog, check the coyotes, then undress to await the next round. Sleep never came, and by five A.M. I lay tense and wide awake. Twice

87

the manager had turned on his light to see what caused the noise, and I was certain he would investigate the next time. It was not a serious situation, but according to my map the next public campground was seventy-five miles south, and at five A.M. I was in no mood to break camp and drive there.

Then I heard howls from wild coyotes—a melody that began soft and low and far away and built to a crescendo of yips and howls that reverberated through our trailer. If Shasta or Rogue answered, its howls would create more immediate response than a dozen dachshunds, and half dressed, I again went to the camper. The coyotes were restless, probably as nervous as I, and I petted and scratched them for several minutes, then returned to bed. In less than half an hour, Peggy was shaking me.

"Wake up," she insisted. "Is there much play in the camper door?"

I groaned.

"No. Listen." She shook me again.

Still groggy, I heard the sounds: a door opening and, after an interval, a gentle slam. I peered through the window above our bed and in the half-light of the approaching dawn realized the cause. When I had last closed the camper door, I had not locked it. Rogue was pushing with his paw, and each time the door swung open it paused momentarily in its arc before closing. He was now too timid to leap through, but when the dachshund returned, as I knew he would, Rogue would change his mind. Images of an escaped coyote raced through my mind, and I ran to the truck, slammed the door with a thud that echoed across the campground, locked it and leaned against the camper, emotionally drained. Surely nothing more could happen to us in Utah.

Across the road a porch light flickered, sending a shaft of bright light toward me. A fat woman opened the door of a mobile home and peered cautiously in one direction and then another. She was wearing a long, flowered robe held tightly at her throat by one hand, and I froze, realizing that in my haste I had forgotten to dress and was standing naked beside the camper. I glided into the shadow of our truck, for at forty-five I was too old to try to cover a somewhat flabby body with a flutter of hands. I held my breath as the woman squinted toward our space. There was a predawn chill in the air, my flesh was erupting with goose bumps and I shivered. Slowly she looked at every vehicle in the park, peering into shadows until my knees were shaking and I wondered if I could remain silent longer. Finally she closed the door and turned off the light and I crept back to our trailer, my teeth chattering uncontrollably. Peggy was laughing.

"And you told *me* not to attract attention," she said.

The next day we were in the heart of Indian land, on the Arizona–New Mexico border near Gallup. The Navajo nation spread north to Colorado and west into Arizona. The Zuni tribe was to the south, and around us were the crumbling pueblos of earlier civilizations. I turned off the Interstate at Thoreau, a small town we could barely see from the highway. A bar, in a half-painted brick building, stood near the exit. A service station was across the intersection, and a store and post office were half a block away. There was little else. Erik's camp was fifteen miles south, remote and difficult to find without a guide. We were to meet him here.

Soon a green station wagon pulled up beside us and Erik stepped out. He waved. Rogue wagged his tail in greeting, and Shasta snorted happily through the wire door. The coyotes were as glad to see him as we were, and suddenly our trip had been worth the effort—even the evening at Lehman Caves, the afternoon in the Cedar Breaks National Monument and the night at Kanab. We had arrived on time, Erik was with us and we could now rest and return home at a leisurely pace. We loaded Erik's gear into the trailer and drove to Bluewater Lake, a state park a few miles south. We were the only campers and were surely guaranteed a trouble-free night. It was a good omen, and I erected the tent and let Shasta and Rogue roam on long chains.

The park was a part of the traditional home of the Indians of the Southwest—Navajo, Zuni and others. The land looked as it must have looked centuries before, and the most visible changes in the Indians were Levi's and trucks. Our camp was beside a dirt road that circled the lake, and pickups passed one after another with families stuffed into every available space. The men wore dark headbands and chambray shirts with their Levi's, and the women wore brightly trimmed skirts. They seemed to be heading toward a small town on the other side of the lake and were in a festive mood. The men waved happily, and we waved back. Sometimes children, riding in the open truck beds, pointed excitedly at Shasta and Rogue.

As we ate dinner in the last rays of day, lights from the town glowed

Peggy and Erik walking Rogue and Shasta at the Arches National Monument.

like stars and jukebox music boomed across the space. The people were celebrating, and even though distance separated us, we felt a part of their festivities. We could hear the low murmur of voices when the music stopped, and then a man began to announce songs over a microphone and the jukebox gave way to live musicians—a guitar, violin and trumpet. I sat beside the truck and Rogue and Shasta lay beside me and together we listened.

The tunes were strange, recognizably Western yet with variations and embellishments that were far more primitive—almost Indian in sound and beat—and from the bank of the lake it was as if the music came to us from the wrong end of a horn. The moon was high, almost overhead, and its light, reflecting cold and white on the water, added an eeriness to the scene. This was country where coyote and Indians had lived in harmony for centuries, and I thought of that now.

To some tribes the coyote was a god and to others a helpful friend. Always their tales told of the heroic things coyotes had done for man. I had collected many tales, and some came back to me as the music echoed across the water and the laughter of the people came as from many children.

In most of the stories I recalled there was only one coyote—the first of his kind, the progenitor of his race—and to the early Navajo this coyote was a god. In the beginning, when the world was covered with water, there were only animals. Coyote was their leader, and one day he sent three diving birds below the water to see what they could find. Two returned empty-handed, but the third had mud in its beak. Coyote took a pawful, patted it round and made the earth.

Then he called the animals of the world to tell them of a new species he planned to create. He said he would call the species Man and asked the animals to describe Man as he should look. Buck felt Man needed large, magnificent antlers. Bear said Man required shaggy fur. Ram insisted Man had to have curved horns. Beaver decided Man should have a broad, flat tail and Owl claimed Man could never survive without wings.

"But if Man is to look like you, why not simply choose one of your young?" Coyote protested. "No, Man must be different. He should have the best qualities of all the animals, not the traits of one or two."

But the animals continued to argue, and Coyote realized they could never agree. He gave each a handful of clay and asked them to make statues of Man as they thought he should look. The animals began to create copies of themselves, and soon it was dark. One by one they fell asleep around the campfire, their work only half completed. Only Coyote remained awake, and when every animal was sleeping he crept through the camp destroying every statue.

Then he molded Man himself, making him a composite of the many animals sleeping beside him. Man stood erect like Bear, had two arms with talons like Eagle and wore fur only on his head, since that was where his brain was. Coyote finished the details as the sky blossomed red and yellow with a new day, and he breathed life into his statue. Then he awakened the other animals so that they could admire his masterpiece —as the animals do to this day.

The story had been told originally by ancestors of the Navajo, but parts have also been traced to California tribes, notably the Miwok. I recalled stories from other tribes, and as the music from across the lake welled loud around us, I remembered a tale of the Plains Indians. To them Coyote was not a deity but a friend.

In the earliest days of the Indians, buffalo had excellent eyesight. They could see the smallest insect half a mile away, and no Indian could stalk close for a kill. Every time men tried to hunt, the animals saw them and moved away. Because there were no other game animals in those days, Indians had very little meat. The Plains tribes hungered for it.

Coyote felt sorry for his friends and tried to devise ways to help and one day had a brilliant idea. He raced into a large herd, kicking up clouds of dirt, and when he was in the center he circled faster and faster until the air was dark and thick. The buffalo's eyes began to water. Soon they could not see, and ever since, the offspring of buffalo have had poor eyesight. Today, even the slowest Indian can hunt them.

Coyote was also a friend of Indians in the Pacific Northwest. A Chinook story tells how the tribe led an idyllic life beside the Columbia River catching the salmon that had been named for the tribe. The fish were then so abundant the Indians did not have to work. They caught great numbers every summer, dried them, smoked them and ate them during the winter.

Sniffing new scents.

But three witches lived at the headwaters of the river and were jealous of the way the Indians lived. The salmon swam to the upper reaches of the river to spawn, and the witches watched silently until the last fish passed, then built a dam, trapping the chinooks high in the mountains. The braves who tired to free the fish were killed by the old women, and soon the tribe was starving.

Coyote decided to help his friends and walked boldly into the witches' camp. In the most polite manner, he told the old ladies they were lucky to own all of the salmon in the world and were perfectly right to refuse to share them. "But," he said, "it must be very difficult to stay awake nights just to protect your fish from the starving wretches below. I will guard them while you rest."

The wrinkled old ladies were very bright and did not believe Coyote, but they lay down on their beds to test him. Soon he proved to be such a diligent watchman that they fell asleep, and when they were snoring, Coyote quietly crept away and began digging at the dam. In the darkness it was difficult to avoid rocks, and soon his paws were bloody and sore, but he kept working because he knew his friends in the valley were hungry. Soon the dam broke, first as a trickle, then as a flood, and Coyote jumped aside. The river rushed through the opening and down the mountain, carrying salmon with it.

The witches leaped to their feet, cursing. One grabbed a long, wicked club with spikes on the end and ran toward Coyote, but he raced swiftly down the mountain. The witches were no match for his speed and soon fell exhausted. Coyote had won, and when he reached the Indian camp he found a great celebration under way. The Indians made him guest of honor.

Another story from the Pacific Northwest tells of a time when there was only one fire in the world. It blazed high on a mountaintop, guarded by three dreadful women called the Skookum Sisters. They refused to share its warmth and tended its blaze day and night.

The sisters were frightening—tall, gaunt and wrinkled, with long legs. Their bodies were covered with the soot and grime of fire, and they were the fastest people on earth. No brave could steal as much as one log, for the sisters could outrun any human.

The winter was very cold. Indians sat huddled beside each other in the chilly forest and looked longingly at the fire far above them, but it gave them no warmth, and young children and old women died, frozen as they slept.

Again Coyote worried and one night crept into the camp of the three sisters. Because he was so stealthy they did not see him until he had a blazing log in his mouth. The oldest sister jumped to her feet shouting, "Catch him!" and the others lunged at him with long knives.

Coyote knew he was not fast enough to outrun the sisters in a straight race and dodged and twisted between the trees, always running downslope just a few feet ahead of the enraged women. The three ran in a fan-shaped formation trying to circle Coyote, but he was very tricky and dodged around and beneath them until he was at the bottom of the mountain.

The Indian camp was now only half a mile ahead, but the race was on flat ground, which gave every advantage to the sisters. They were gaining with every step, and Coyote ran as fast as he could, but he could not open his mouth to breathe because he would drop the log, and soon there were only inches separating Coyote and the fastest of the sisters. The woman knew she had to reach Coyote before he reached the Indians or lose control of fire forever, and she lunged at Coyote, her sooty hand outstretched. She caught his tail, and Coyote spun through the air, crashing against the ground still clutching the blazing log in his mouth. The other sisters closed in. Soon they would have him and kill him, even though he twisted, kicked and scratched to break free.

Suddenly Coyote turned, twisting his body into an arc, and plunged the blazing log against the hand of the sister who held him. The woman screamed and released her hold, and Coyote leaped to his feet just before the others reached him. He raced into the Indians' camp, and as he reached it the evil spell was broken. The sisters returned to the mountain defeated.

The Indians made a giant fire. By its blazing light they saw the black print of a sooty hand on Coyote's tail, but nothing they could do would remove the stain. To this day coyotes wear the mark of the Skookum Sisters as a badge of honor.

Some New Mexican tribes tell stories that characterize coyotes as neither gods nor friends, but as mischievous animals who play troublesome but harmless pranks on people. One of these is Peggy's favorite, and I thought of it as we listened to the music.

An important chief was given the job of putting stars into the heavens. There were more than one thousand, and he stacked them neatly in a basket, removed them one at a time and placed them precisely in the sky in even rows. The chief was a very meticulous and pompous man, and the harder he worked the more ridiculous the situation seemed to Coyote. He could not understand why stars had to be placed precisely when nothing else in nature was positioned that way. He could control himself no longer and darted toward the chief, tipping the basket as he ran. The stars tumbled across the sky in all directions, settling in a hundred random patterns, and Coyote rolled on the grass in laughter. That is the way the Milky Way was made.

The first time Peggy heard the story, her eyes widened. "I believe it. Shasta could have done that," she said.

Still other stories came to me, and suddenly I realized that only the white man's tales made the coyote a killer. To the white man coyotes were cowardly, tricky and worthless, but to the red man he was an animal who helped them and taught them to live a better life. Either the white man or the red man was wrong, and as Shasta and Rogue slept at my feet, I knew the problem had to be with the white man. The red man had known coyotes for centuries.

The earliest Southwestern Indians were apartment builders, and all that remains of their civilizations is the ruins. The people were the ancestors of Pueblo Indians, the Hopi of northern Arizona and the Zuni of western New Mexico, the original storytellers whose tales I recalled. Some buildings were erected more than a thousand years ago—places since occupied by alien nomads, Navajo, Ute and Apache, who cannot recall, even in collective tribal memory, those first mysterious constructors. Sometime around the eleventh century climates changed; there were long, severe droughts and what had been a lush, green, fertile valley became a barren desert. The apartment dwellers moved on, perhaps to oblivion.

We stopped in Farmington, New Mexico, to see the Aztec Ruins, a pueblo village misnamed by European explorers. It was once a three-story apartment complex, and the Giant Kiva, a huge circular building forty-eight feet in diameter, had been restored. It was cavelike, with

Shasta sleeping outside.

cool, earthen walls. Our voices echoed mysteriously when we talked, and we stood where tribal ceremonies had once been held.

Hovenweap National Monument, on the Colorado–Utah border, is a similar but smaller complex, less restored but more dramatic, on the edge of a hill. Like all of the ruins in the Southwest, Hovenweap is earthen brown in color, and under a brilliant, warm sun its hues contrast against an intensely blue sky spotted with white clouds in a scene duplicated in no other part of the nation. The coyotes were as interested in new scents as we were in new scenes and never protested the long hours of travel. Each evening, Peggy and Erik walked them as I made camp.

We ran out of dog food at Hovenweap, and the grocery in a small town near the monument stocked only fish-flavored cat food. Erik looked at it in disgust, but Peggy scooped several cans into her arms. "Books say coyotes will eat anything," she insisted.

With the food on board, we camped in the desert near Hovenweap. We were in high desert country, open land with sand and sage—a site similar to the one at Fallon, Nevada—and the coyotes were relaxed and calm. They were chained to the trailer at opposite ends so that they could run without tangling. Rogue sniffed the unopened food with obvious interest, and Peggy smiled triumphantly.

Erik opened the cans and emptied two each into their feeding bowls. Shasta trotted eagerly to hers, sniffed, then turned away. She looked questioningly at Erik as if to ask if it was truly edible, then came back to try again. The instant her nose touched the food she backed away in disgust and, turning around, kicked dirt into the bowl until the offending meal was completely buried. Rogue smelled his plate tentatively, backed away, edged forward cautiously as if the unappealing mound were dangerous and sniffed. Then he lifted his leg above the mess and, flipping the pan with one paw, also buried it.

"I'd call that a decisive vote," Erik said.

That night we shared our dinner with the coyotes and left the contents of the cans on the desert for other animals. Peggy thought the local residents would not be as finicky as our coyotes.

When we pulled out of Reno on the final leg of our return journey, I grew uneasy. California funnels border traffic into official inspection stations where officers check food and agricultural items for undesirable bacteria and insects. At this time, they also inspected certain animals to verify that they had been vaccinated against rabies and distemper. The men had the authority to refuse admission to any car with items considered "unsafe," and it was for this solitary encounter with the California law that our coyotes had been inoculated.

It was dark, nearly midnight, when I saw the lights of the inspection station ahead, and they grew larger as Peggy hurriedly dug through my wallet to find the receipt from Dr. Evers. I'd put it there when we left home because it was proof that our coyotes complied with state law. Without the papers, we had been told, we would face a long, agonizing delay. She was still fumbling with a tangle of papers when I reached the station.

A man came out and asked, "Where have you been?"

I told him, and he leaned close with a deeper interest. Longer trips usually meant souvenirs, although we had none, and souvenirs meant things to inspect.

"Bring back plants, food or agricultural products?" he asked.

When I answered "no" to every question, his eyes narrowed with disbelief. Peggy was still sorting through my papers, and the man watched her intently.

Then he asked, "Cotton blankets? Buy any cotton products in Arizona or New Mexico?"

Again my answer was "no," and again there was a look of mistrust on his face. Peggy still had not found the certificate. The man turned to the camper.

"What are these?" he demanded.

I told him coyotes, and he peered through the window, hands rimming his face to shield his eyes against the outside light. Rogue cringed against the wall, but Shasta held her ground, baring her teeth to prove authority didn't bother her. Their eyes met momentarily as neither coyote nor inspector moved. Then the man turned to me.

"They bite?" he asked.

"Very much." I nodded. The man looked at me, then at the coyotes, and slowly, for the first time, smiled. His arm came up abruptly and he waved us through. I stepped on the gas. Peggy still hadn't found the paper.

"How do you figure that?" I asked incredulously. "All the effort with Shasta and Dr. Evers was unnecessary. All Shasta had to do was show her teeth."

I looked in the rearview mirror, and in the fading light from the inspection station I could see Shasta's yellow eyes sparkling and it was as if she were laughing. Home was only an hour away, and together the five of us had traveled nearly three thousand miles.

Chapter Ten

A MEXICAN PROVERB CLAIMS, "God made coyotes to drive men mad," and in December I realized living with two coyotes does demand a touch of insanity.

At dawn on the fourth day of that month, large, wet flakes of snow fell through the trees, and Shasta's gentle whine awoke Erik. She was sitting below his window, and Rogue was behind her, leaping, kicking and scattering snow in the yard. The deep snow had drifted to the top of the run, and the coyotes had escaped.

Erik called to me and I ran outside, a shirt thrown hastily over my pajamas. Shasta rolled over, her tail thumping happily, and I carried her to the house. Rogue came just close enough so that I could almost touch him; then he ran away, twisting and turning joyously as I floundered behind, the snow working down the tops of my slippers like icy fingers. It was useless to give chase, and I stopped, waist-deep in snow. My legs were cold and my feet were icy, but I waited. Rogue came again, trying to lure me into his game, inching closer and closer cautiously, and when he was at arm's length I lunged, hooking a thumb through his collar. He was put in the house with Shasta.

Erik and I cleared the snow from the run and put both animals inside. Minutes later Shasta was free, racing toward us a second time. She rolled over in front of Erik, and he picked her up and carried her back to the run. Three more times she escaped, ran to Erik and was returned to the run. Getting out had become a game.

There were no holes in the fence, no way beneath the wire or door, and the snowdrift used to escape the first time was gone. I could see no avenues of freedom, yet Shasta had found one. Why not Rogue? That was the strangest part. I watched the run half hidden by a porch pillar like a spy in a very poor movie, but Shasta knew she was being observed and stared back coldly until I turned away in shame. Then, in the instant when my head was averted, she was free, running toward me, grinning as she came.

It was maddening to be tricked by a coyote, and I put her into the run a fourth time and circled slowly, assuming a very professional air. Shasta followed step by step as if challenging me to detect her system. Everything seemed in order, and there was no visible route—until she leaped to the top of her house to watch me better, and suddenly I knew the answer. Shasta was standing on the snow-covered roof looking *over* the fence. How stupid I had been! Snow added sufficient height to raise her above the wire. All she had to do was step out. And it explained why Rogue did not follow. He had climbed out the first time because it was gentle and easy, but he disliked heights and refused to follow his sister over the new route. I removed snow from the roof and stretched a wire across the top as a further precaution.

Later, we took the coyotes walking in snow and found Erik and his friend John Selberg building a round-bellied snowman in the yard. We watched as the boys rolled giant snowballs, placing one above the other. They began making a round face at the top, and when the eyes and mouth went in Shasta became interested. She sniffed the air, pulled hard against her leash and dragged me forward. I could not tell what excited her, but when she reached the snowman she leaped high, landing with a vanilla cookie in her mouth. Erik had used the cookie for the mouth, and the snowman now stood with half a face.

Winter is a difficult time for wild coyotes. Game is scarce, and in snow the act of stalking prey becomes difficult. Coyotes are easily seen against snow because of their color; walking, running and leaping are harder, slower and more exhausting and a wild coyote must increase the size of his territory to survive. In winter more than in any other season, he becomes a "scavenger of the forest," eating the things he can find. The killing of deer, elk and moose occurs occasionally, but stories are

Erik made a snowman and Shasta discovered the joy of jumping against it.

Erik and Peggy with the coyotes.

exaggerated. Most coyotes discovered dining on these animals are actually feeding on game that has become snowbound, weakened and exhausted by winter and too close to death to survive.

Other coyotes live by adapting their winter diet to unexpected offerings. In parts of the West, ranchers feed range cattle cottonseed cakes —a nourishing, even good-tasting compound—which are scattered over the feeding area. Coyotes probably discovered the attraction as soon as it was introduced, and although it is not used as often as in the past, it is still not uncommon to see coyotes feeding calmly among the herds. They are with the cattle not to kill, but to share in the feast.

In still other areas, coyotes have established a symbiotic relationship with species they usually ignore. In Yellowstone National Park, for example, coyotes use buffalo to help survive the winters. They do not harass or kill them, but simply follow in the tracks of the huge, shaggy beasts. Coyotes have discovered that the wide, cloven hoofs and browsing habits of buffalo will level even the deepest snowdrifts, and walking in buffalo tracks is easier than fighting snow. Moreover, when buffalo browse they root out mice, and coyotes standing almost beneath the buffalo's feet can easily catch them.

For our coyotes, living in the winter was even better than in summer, for they were in the house more. They ate well, but had individual tastes and different ways of savoring meals. One night we gave them vanilla ice cream laced with nuts, and Rogue tackled his with quick and obvious pleasure, growling often to be certain Shasta did not steal any. In contrast, Shasta ate her portion slowly and methodically, pausing between mouthfuls. I found this curious and went over to investigate. She was carefully removing all the nuts. Several were piled neatly beside her plate.

Their winter coats are thick and warm.

On another night, we gave them pieces of hard candy—the type scattered about the house in bowls for the holiday season. Rogue downed his rapidly, and we heard the crunch of his strong jaws as the candy splintered in many pieces, disappearing in one gulp; but again, Shasta stood apart, rolling her candy gently in her mouth. Her eyes were closed; she was savoring the flavor and making each piece last as long as possible.

The coyotes were now rarely destructive, even though there were many things in the house to tempt them, but there was one exception. Magazines were piled high on the coffee table, publications Peggy or I planned to read. Shasta would occasionally sniff them and turn away, but once monthly she seemed drawn to the stack as iron is drawn to a magnet. At that time she explored the pile carefully with her nose until she found a special magazine and if we were not watching would jerk it from the pile and tear it apart page by page.

The magazine was *Réalitiés*, printed in France. It carried some scent, in paper or ink, that I could not detect, and even when it was hidden she always found it. Nothing else in the pile interested her, and when *Réalitiés* was missing, she left the stack alone.

"I should write to the editors," I suggested. "They may not know the broad appeal of their publication."

The coyotes were full grown, with a rich winter pelage, and their woolly fur stood out from their bodies. It made them seem larger, like stuffed toys. Their coats were now buff-colored, with patches of orange on their legs and ears, and the black accents—the print of the Skookum Sisters—stood out on their backs and tails. Their stomachs were white.

As I watched them one evening, I remembered that for more than one hundred years hunters have killed coyotes for their fur. As early as 1850 the pelts had commercial value, selling for a dollar or two and used as trim on jackets and coats. The demand rose and fell with fashion, but in the retail trade they were considered inferior to all other furs and were sold under various names that disguised their origin. Many furriers called them "local wolf," and even the conservative, honorable Hudson's Bay Company refused to call coyote hides by their true name. Hudson's Bay furs were described as "cased wolf," which referred to the method by which the animal was skinned. When I was in college, pieces of coy-

Our coyotes are in the house more in winter than in summer.

ote pelt, especially the tail, billowed from the antennae of cars, and in 1947 there was a surprising, booming postwar market. Three thousand pelts were sold in one Western state. Today's market, thankfully, is not large, but the fur is still used commercially as trim on jackets and other clothing, and as always, the prime season for fur hunters is winter.

Coyote fur has two distinct layers: an outer one of coarse guard hairs and an inner one of fine, close wool. The guard hairs remain the year around, but the wool thins in summer and thickens in winter, and now Shasta and Rogue were "winterized." Their inner fur had grown so thick it was difficult to part. Even on the coldest nights it retained body heat, and Rogue often preferred to sleep outside his house in snow-drifts. The experience never seemed to bother him, and he always awoke well rested. In driving rain, their fur shed water like a raincoat, and when they came into the house after a storm the guard hairs would be soaked yet the inner fur was seldom more than damp. Their skin was always dry, and even the wettest fur dried in minutes.

Winter was also a time when we heard new coyote stories. Many visitors had tales for us, some serious and some humorous. One of the best came from Chet Miller, an Oregon horseman and Peggy's cousin. The coyotes were in the house, and as Chet talked, Shasta remained aloof and detached, lying in one corner, but Rogue actually seemed interested.

"I was riding my horse on top of a high mesa. The wind was coming strong over the edge from the desert, blowing so hard you couldn't hear a sound," Chet said. "Suddenly I saw a coyote sitting on the edge, probably enjoying the view. He was a big fellow, about the size of Rogue."

At the mention of his name Rogue pressed closer, looking attentively into Chet's face as if the best of the story were to come. Chet continued, "The coyote couldn't hear or smell me because the wind blew against him, and I tied my horse to a bush and tiptoed close until I stood directly behind the fellow. He was concentrating on something, and I prodded his backside with my boot, asking, "What in hell you looking at?" The animal jumped straight into the air, turned sideways without touching ground and hit the earth running. He was out of sight in less than one minute."

We began laughing, Chet hardest of all, and Rogue turned away in disgust, walked to Shasta's side and lay down with an audible groan. Nothing we could say would bring him back to our group, and it was almost as if Rogue knew we were making fun of coyotes. Later, when I tried to pet him, he walked away.

Chapter Eleven

SINCE EARLIEST MEMORY, coyotes have been hunted—for pelts, because they were said to kill cattle and finally because they supposedly slaughtered sheep. Yet when the profit was removed from pelts, and it was proved that coyotes kill neither cattle nor sheep in substantial numbers (but live mostly on rodents, rabbits, snakes and insects), the killing of them continued.

Why? Because few people understand a coyote, and his life has little value. An Arizona woolgrower told me he would pay happily to exterminate the species. A stocky Colorado rancher boasted that he had killed seven hundred and fifty, and he said that more would die. A raging Utah sheepherder threatened to shoot me because I had two, and in Maine the carcass of a male coyote was displayed in a square in the small village of Millinocket. It hung like a witch in Old Salem, and villagers gathered shouting, cursing and throwing rocks. State Representative Roswell Dyer was so excited he placed a bill before the legislature offering a fifty-dollar bounty for other coyotes killed in the state. The incongruity: this was the first such animal seen in forty years, the species was nearly unknown in New England and there had been no reported problems.

In the Midwest, a man told me, "We used to hunt the wheat fields. Sometimes we walked the furrows, pushing game ahead, shooting rabbits, birds and coyotes. Other times we went after coyotes alone, sixty

DANGER!
Poisoned Cartridges in the Area!

ESE CARTRIDGES ARE DANGEROUS.
EY CONTAIN DEADLY CYANIDE.
AY AWAY AND KEEP YOUR DOGS
VAY.

¡PELIGRO!
¡Cartuchos Venenosos en Esta Localidad!

ESTOS CARTUCHOS SON PELIGROSOS.
CONTIENEN CIANURO, UN VENENO
FATAL.
PERSONAS CON PERROS FUERA DE ESTA
ZONA.

Many Americans believe coyotes are born to be killed. Predator-control signs are common in our area, as in other sheep-raising sections of the West.

farmers coming together from the corners of a field, and in the center we killed as many as one hundred."

Peggy was astonished. "Why?" she asked. "They ate rabbits and mice—animals that ruined your crops."

The fellow blinked. "We never thought of coyotes except as targets."

If there is an easy explanation for anticoyote hostility, the man hit on it in one word: targets. The woolgrower, rancher and sheepherder, the townspeople in Millinocket, the farmer in the Midwest and others across the country count coyotes among that number of animals born only to be killed. It is a gut judgment based on an archaic concept of "bad animals," and a species makes that list because it has, or supposedly has, posed a threat to man, his westward expansion, his pasture, his crops, his chickens, cattle or sheep. Many are included—fox, wolf, coyote, bear, mountain lion, badger, weasel, mouse, hawk, snakes and more. The outmoded canon decrees "bad" animals must die, and die they do.

For years the major killers have been hired federal guns, men of the Branch of Predator and Rodent Control, a part of the Fish and Wildlife Service. Until recently they disposed of nearly one hundred thousand coyotes annually. Now, in a major organizational shakeup, the name has been changed—to the Division of Wildlife Services. Only the game remains the same.

Division of Wildlife Services employees still work with state governments, and in California, where I live, the arrangement is typical. Agents, backed by a slush fund of federal, state and local money, fan out to "problem" areas and, alone or with county agents, work to eradicate predators. In recent years the California budget has been close to one million dollars annually (most of the sum is spent in sheep-raising communities), and sheep growers give the impression they will be driven out of business if it is not met. Yet when the facts are in, the program, whether judged on the basis of the "threat," the cattle and sheep "saved" or even on the number of coyotes killed, becomes difficult to justify.

Shasta and Rogue.

Coyotes can be a problem, but the blame is often misplaced or over-emphasized. Near Chandler, Arizona, a pack of wild animals swept across the land killing more than a hundred sheep. Near Dodge City, Kansas, another pack stormed through farm fields slaughtering newborn calves. And near Athens, Georgia, a young man was attacked and nearly killed as he walked in the woods.

In each case experts sagely advised, "Coyotes did it"; and in each case it was later proved coyotes had not. Proof came, in Georgia, when the young man was attacked a second time and managed to kill his assailant—a German shepherd. In Arizona, Kansas and most other states, similar packs of marauding dogs are often mistakenly identified as coyotes. In one state more than three hundred thousand wild dogs run free, and the havoc they spread is more than that caused by all wild animals.

When coyotes are the culprits (for they are predators and kill to survive), the problem is generally exaggerated. Sheep men officially claim losses to coyotes as between 7 and 12 percent a year—the percentage depending on the area and the sheep men you talk with; but impartial experts have publicly stated the true figure is less than 3 percent. Many more sheep are lost through poor lambing practices, improper herding, winter dangers and shipping.

Yet prejudice remains, and if you venture west any summer beyond the tourist-packed streets of Las Vegas and the dude ranches of Colorado, you can see it in the way coyotes are hunted and treated. Animals have been found with their jaws wired closed, or purposely broken to prevent eating, and some have been trapped and left alone—both unnecessary, slow, difficult deaths; others have been scalped for bounty, then released alive, an even more inhumane treatment; and still others have been gunned from low-flying planes, dynamited or poisoned—all inaccurate, hit-or-miss propositions. Both Cleveland Amory, in his book *Man Kind?*, and Jack Olsen, in *Slaughter the Animals, Poison the Earth*, have thoroughly documented man's insidious efforts to exterminate the coyote. The campaign is devastating.

For more than a century strychnine has been the traditional executioner, most often mixed with squares of tallow or lard and occasionally injected into eggs. Cyanide has also been traditional, and a popular device has been the coyote-getter, a gunlike mechanism with a cyanide-filled

cartridge, buried with a square of fur or felt aboveground. The curious, who come to investigate, are shot in the face. But the most effective has been 1080, sodium fluoracetate, a deadly poison developed during World War II. It is odorless, tasteless and colorless; can be dissolved in water, mixed with grain, injected in freshly killed game or put in squares of meat; and once in the body causes fear, panic, excitement and finally hypersensitivity. A poisoned animal may run for miles in panic, until death comes mercifully, and a second animal, feeding on the first, can also be poisoned. As many as five animals, each dining on the carcass of a predecessor, can be poisoned by the dreadful chain reaction; 1080 is unrelenting.

These programs are costly and inefficient, since the poisons are excessively expensive and nonselective. Many other animals, neither "target" predators nor dangerous to man, have been killed. In 1972 the nationwide program cost Americans more than eight million dollars, and for that sum a combination of professionals and amateurs spread poison across the land like butter, killing more than 189,000 animals. Included were 89,000 coyotes, 24,270 foxes, 20,780 bobcats, 10,800 skunks, 7,600 opossums, 6,950 badgers, 2,770 red wolves, 1,170 beavers and 840 bears. A substantial number of the species were not predators, and some, such as the red wolf, are on the endangered-species list. In addition, a surprising number of household pets and some humans have been killed throughout the years.

For these reasons and after extensive efforts by a number of conservation groups, President Nixon banned the use of predator poisons on public lands in February, 1972. His plan was vehemently opposed (and has been since) by the National Wool Growers Association. Partly as a result of their lobbying, poisons have been permitted on private land, even the dangerous 1080 (used not long ago in California). Now the Environmental Protection Agency promises to rescind the Presidential order by permitting Western ranchers to use cyanide coyote-getters on public lands for a year or more, in a new war against the coyote.

The turnabout is unnecessary. "Shotgun" poisoning techniques are neither desirable nor essential, and nothing explains the reasoning better than the "Leopold Report," a government-backed study made several years ago by a number of famous scientists (Dr. A. Starker Leopold,

University of California; Dr. Ira Gabrielson, U.S. Government; Dr. Clarence Cottam, Dr. Stanley Cain and Thomas Kimball, National Wildlife Federation).

Their report, "Predator Control in the United States," recommends sweeping changes in the way we consider and control predators. It calls loudly for less slaughter and more concern and says, "Native animals are *not* in danger from native predators."

The study warns, "Far more animals are being killed [as predators] than would be required for the effective protection of livestock, agricultural crops, wildland resources and human welfare. As a consequence, many animals which have never offended property owners or public resources are being killed unnecessarily."

There are more humane ways to solve the problem of predators, and solutions should include implementation of the recommendations in the Leopold Report, as well as stricter control over poisons. The private use of strychnine, cyanide and 1080 should be banned; when the use of one of these poisons is required, it should be only under rigid, expert supervision. County, state and federal trappers are an important part of any program, but their enthusiasm for killing must be curbed. Control should be the key, and animals should be killed only after guilt has been established, and only when absolutely essential. "Shotgun" poisoning eradicates many predators in an effort to hit one and is not justified.

One alternative has been proved in Missouri. Years ago, officials decided mass poisonings were not only inhumane, but unwise, and under a new program officials work with farmers on specific damage claims without distinction as to the wildlife involved. Damages caused by deer are treated exactly like those caused by raccoons and coyotes: the troublemaker is trapped and transferred to another area, and only when that is impossible is he killed. In the time the program has been in effect, losses have been reduced dramatically.

"Farmers don't chase imaginary predators as they used to do," one Missouri official said.

Finally, we must make room for predators. Their presence in the wildlife system is important to us and to the balance of nature. In short, we must learn to appreciate our smallest native wolf.

In Canada, the Ontario government offers an unusual attraction at

Rogue

the Algonquin Provincial Park: a "howling safari," a very popular night-time nature walk. On warm, moonlit evenings, as many as a thousand people have stood at the edge of a lone canyon to hear night animals and have been treated to the tremulous, reverberating howls of timber wolves.

We can do similar things in our state and national parks. J. Frank Dobie, a famous writer, teacher and champion of coyotes, was the first man to suggest wilderness "hearing places," and he was right. We should establish zones where coyotes may live and develop tours so that the people of our cities can hear their songs. The sound of a coyote at night is as natural as any in the forest, and without his call, carried on a rush of wind, we can hear only a part of nature.

Chapter Twelve

One winter evening Peggy asked, "How many puppies will Shasta have?"

"None if we depend on Rogue," I replied.

"He was backward," she admitted, "but he was young."

And Peggy was right. Our coyotes were now two years old, and while Shasta had seemed eager to mate the year before, Rogue had not. His reluctance had been normal, however, since coyotes rarely breed their first year. Oestrum, the period of fertility, comes annually, and coyotes generally conceive in January and deliver in March. We were approaching that time again.

The idea of our coyotes having pups appealed to us. Peggy had a woman's maternalistic sympathy, a concern for diet and comfort, and offered Shasta special foods and warm, soft places. I was simply excited by the prospect of pups, curious to know what coyotes one generation removed from the wild would be like. Only Erik totally opposed the idea. He was convinced that two coyotes in a family were enough.

The fact that the parents came from a single litter bothered many friends. They warned that inbreeding—the mating of closely related animals—was dangerous. Some insisted we would produce uncontrollable killers, and others believed such recessive qualities as undershot jaws, cataracts and deformed bones would result.

We didn't believe them, but since I knew little about genetics, I

The idea of our coyotes having puppies was appealing, but human encouragement did little to effect successful mating.

questioned Dr. Evers. "Inbreeding can affect physical characteristics," he said, "but it takes several generations and many litters to create most abnormalities. Recessive qualities won't show in early pups, and there is no such a thing as a born killer. If Shasta has a single pregnancy, there is little danger."

Oestrum unexpectedly came early—in December. It was difficult to believe, since it was one month early, but we knew that captivity, diet and other factors occasionally altered schedules. Yet if we were convinced, Rogue was not. The serious boy-girl relationship I expected seemed totally lacking.

We had read about Rick Dyson, curator of mammals at the Arizona-Sonora Desert Museum near Tucson. The doctor had successfully bred rare desert wolves, and I decided to ask for advice. When I reached him by phone, Dyson explained, "Her period should last three or four weeks, and the critical time when she can conceive occurs during the second week. Not all animals mature at similar rates, and your male may need a push. Ask your veterinarian about methyl testosterone, a male hormone I've used on wolves. It works."

At the beginning of the second week, I gave Rogue a small white tablet in a marshmallow. It was testosterone, and according to instructions, I was to give him one daily for a week. Its impact was surprising and quick. He came into the house for dinner one hour later and between bites leaped back nervously to sweep the ceiling with a frightened gaze, as if he expected catastrophe to befall him. He had never done this before, and additional tablets only increased his apprehension. On the fifth night, when I dropped a book, he scurried sideways the length of the room. He was wound as tightly as a spring, yet showed little interest in Shasta.

"The poor fellow will fly apart before he has an opportunity to become a father," I predicted. I stopped giving him tablets.

There was still hope. Coyotes are dedicated parents. Their urge to mate is strong, and in the wild they gather as oestrum approaches and pair off for breeding. While not mating for life, as stories claim, couples often remain together for years.

The female prepares a series of dens—usually enlarging existing places such as badger and rabbit holes, but occasionally utilizing ready-made sites such as caves, culverts and even abandoned homes. Shelter is secondary to seclusion. Places are chosen for a view of the surrounding country, and the vantage point is more important than the condition of a den. Water is not essential, since the young suckle, and dens have been found six miles from the closest water source. A most unusual den was discovered in a tree. Its quarters were cramped, and it was even more surprising because the opening was five feet aboveground.

The female continues to build dens until a few days before her pups are whelped, and by that time she may have prepared as many as ten. There are several reasons for so many changing sites; cleanliness and safety are the most obvious. A mother cleans her den often so that it will neither attract insects nor have a scent to draw predators. When one site becomes dirty, she moves her family to a new one. Many coyote watchers claim that once a den is discovered the mother moves her young, but a number of authentic studies indicate this is not an inflexible rule. Some mothers have raised families in dens that have been disturbed, and others have abandoned both den and pups for personal safety.

A female usually delivers four to ten pups, although litters may number as many as twenty. New-born coyotes are blind, and their eyes remain closed for ten or more days. They are kept in the darkened den and emerge after the third week. When they are one month old the parents begin survival training, and the pups are taught to track, hunt, kill and hide.

Shasta's strange cycle added a perplexing dimension to our winter. It ended abruptly during the second week, then began again three weeks later, in mid-January, about the proper and expected time. If the first had been false oestrum, not an uncommon occurrence, could we be certain the second was true? Perhaps I had been impatient, and I felt doubly guilty since I had obviously subjected Rogue to the hallucinating effects of testosterone for nothing.

He behaved differently now; he was more positive, possessive and aggressive. Malcolm and Julie visited us, and we brought the coyotes into the house to greet them. Rogue attached himself to Julie, excluding everyone else and following her closely. When it was time to dine we put them into the run and carried their dinners to them. Malcolm had one pan, and when he stepped into the run Rogue met him snarling and

Rogue and the author. The trust and friendship of our coyotes have made it impossible to return them to the wild.

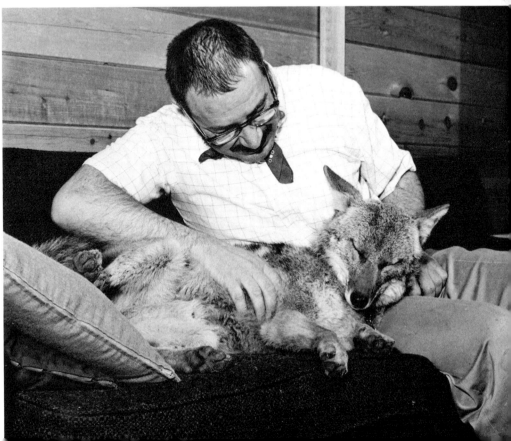

growling. Malcolm put the food on the ground and retreated, and Rogue calmed instantly. He came to me to be petted.

I told Malcolm, "It must be part of the mating game. He may think you're competing for Shasta. Perhaps he's getting the idea after all."

Shasta became affectionate, whining softly when Rogue was near and digging her muzzle into the fur on his back. Sometimes he answered with tiny, gentle bites, and to me the moments seemed tender, or at least a coyote's equivalent of tender; yet Rogue's advances never advanced. Concerned friends offered many suggestions. Some told us to give him hot baths; others suggested oysters; one said a certain cure was ground antelope horn and another told us to chain Shasta outside where a wild coyote could mate with her. The chain was ruled out instantly as unnecessarily cruel and dangerous; the hot bath was eliminated on the basis of practicality—no one wanted to give Rogue one—and the aphrodisiacs were considered to be only folklore. For better or worse, our chances lay with instinct.

We had been told the proper way to guarantee mating was to separate the animals, bringing them together after a long separation. I knew the system worked for breeding fish, but the logistics were difficult. Rogue had to be kept in the house while Shasta remained in the run, and when we tried it all that happened was that Shasta became lonely. She howled continually until Rogue was returned—yet when he did return, nothing happened.

As the second week progressed, Rogue seemed more aware of Shasta. She nuzzled him more, whining and biting, and they played often. Occasionally during moments of play Rogue would embrace her from behind with his paws, but when he did she simply collapsed. He sailed over her head, a bewildered smile on his face as if he were demanding to know if this was truly the way the thing was supposed to go.

But one evening he seemed most determined, following Shasta, pawing and growling with mock ferocity. The two played wildly, then tired and rested, and I gave each a piece of candy. Rogue devoured his instantly, but Shasta stood apart, her eyes closed as she rolled the candy in her mouth. Without warning, Rogue leaped on Shasta's back. He suddenly seemed to realize what nature demanded. Shasta's eyes opened in surprise; the candy fell from her mouth and rolled across the floor end over end and Rogue watched, fascinated. He could stand it no longer, deserted Shasta and greedily devoured the candy. There were no more attempts to mate.

But one day Shasta began to dig. The perimeter of their run was covered with concrete to keep the wire fence in place, but the center had been left barren, and soon that area was dotted with holes, three large enough for Shasta to disappear into. Perhaps mating had occurred when we were not aware of it. To me the digging seemed meaningful.

It was too early to be certain. The first stages of canine gestation occur unnoticed. Full development requires sixty to sixty-five days, as with dogs, but the obvious, certain signs, such as increased girth and enlarged breasts, do not appear until the second month. By late February it was obvious Shasta was not pregnant. Her digging, which lasted three weeks, had been prompted only by instinct.

We were disappointed but not unhappy as we took them walking that spring. Trees were greening, the earth was regenerating for a new summer and the time ahead offered still another opportunity. We rested on a stump beside the stream that passes near our home, and Peggy stroked Shasta's head. She told her, "You're the best."

Rogue nuzzled close to me for similar encouragement, and I said gently, "If that's true, then you're second best, but don't worry. Next January just try a little harder."

Rogue licked my face with a warm, wet tongue.

Shasta did not conceive the next winter or the winter after that, and we concluded that the conditions of captivity played some part in her reluctance to become a mother. Quite possibly, hers was an unconscious reaction to the unnaturalness of her situation; in the wild, she might have borne several litters.

We waited and watched in anticipation, but we were neither impatient nor truly disappointed that Shasta and Rogue had not mated successfully. When I had brought them home as small puppies years before, I realized we had removed them forever from their natural ways. They could not be returned to the wild, as some animals in captivity had been, because the coyote is relentlessly hunted by man and we had taken from them their one defense—suspicion.

125

While neither Shasta nor Rogue was friendly with all people, they had learned to trust man and not to fear him. In the wild, that combination could cost them their lives. To set them free would be to sentence them to death; and as pleasant as it might be to dream of a day when they could return to nature, it was the one thing I could never give them.